100

2nd Edition

THINGS TO DO IN
SALT LAKE CITY
BEFORE YOU
DIE

D0557161

Try #25

everydyamite
insta twitter

JEREMY PUGH

REEDY PRESS

Library of Congress Control Number: 9781681061948

ISBN: 2018962446

Design by Jill Halpin

Cover Image:
Photo courtesy Utah Office of Tourism
Mesa Arch in Canyonlands National Park

Printed in the United States of America
19 20 21 22 23 5 4 3 2 1

Please note that websites, phone numbers, addresses, and company names are subject to change or cancellation. We did our best to relay the most accurate information available, but due to circumstances beyond our control, please do not hold us liable for misinformation. When exploring new destinations, please do your homework before you go.

DEDICATION

This book is dedicated to the memory of Glen Warchol,
a true newsman, mentor, friend, and all-around bad ass.
We miss you Papa Warchol.

• •

CONTENTS

● ●

• •

Sports and Recreation

● ●

Culture and History

● ●

Shopping and Fashion

PREFACE

Salt Lake City has always been a unique, even peculiar place. Home to the world headquarters of the Church of Jesus Christ of Latter-Day Saints (the LDS Church or, informally, the Mormons), the LDS pioneers came to Salt Lake in 1847 after a long and dangerous trek across the Great Plains. Once they arrived, they literally built this city.

For a long time, that's pretty much what most folks knew about Utah, but slowly and quietly the old Salt Lake City began to give way to what I call new Salt Lake City. As with any place so richly steeped in history, to understand the roots of change you have to go way, way, way back. In the late 1800s, federal troops stationed in Utah discovered rich veins of copper and silver, paving the way for the age of the silver barons and outside influence. The east-west railroad brought an influx of laborers who would add diversity in both faith and Mormon-defined vice to the mix, and Utah's admission to the United States in 1896 brought even more changes. Still, Utah remained apart with a dominant religion, which often dictated politics and individual conscience. Those old mining claims would become privately owned ski resorts, and the jet set had a reason to skip Colorado. Finally, the 2002 Winter Olympics cast aside the veil and shone a light on it all—Mormons, gentiles, sinners, and saints—at the base of a vast outdoor playground.

Salt Lake City is the center of it all. A clean, walkable, bikeable city with a progressive city government, our city attracts talented and creative people from all over the world who see Salt Lake City as a blank canvas. The food scene has exploded, as has the nightlife. Art, music, and creativity are flourishing in what was once considered a sleepy backwater.

• •

It's an amazing time to live in Salt Lake City. A sense of energy and optimism prevails that is fueled by the imposing Central Wasatch Mountain Range that towers over our city and is essentially our communal backyard. Salt Lakers are an active bunch. We hike, we bike, we climb, we ski, we snowboard, and that mountain culture affects just about every aspect of life here.

The list in this book is by no means comprehensive. Salt Lake City occupies only a small area of the larger Great Salt Lake Valley and Wasatch Front and Back, so not necessarily everything on this list applies for an SLC zip code. After more than twenty years of watching and writing about this evolving place, however, I've compiled what I consider an essential checklist to appreciate the 801.

I'd love to hear what you think about my selections and of your adventures as you move through the list. You can find me @verydynamite on Twitter and Instagram.

Happy travels!
Jeremy Pugh

ACKNOWLEDGMENTS

First, I would like to thank Shawn Stinson at Visit Salt Lake, who recommended me to Reedy Press for this project. I'd also like to thank Mary Brown Malouf, whose friendship, humor and support keeps life in Salt Lake interesting.

I owe a deep debt of gratitude to all my Salt Lake friends and colleagues who chimed in with ideas for this book. I am surrounded by people who love living in Salt Lake City, and their vibrant participation in everything our city offers helps make this a wonderful place. To everyone who has given me the outlets to write about this city and state for more than a decade (Salt Lake magazine, Visit Salt Lake, Utah Office of Tourism, *Sunset*, *SKI* magazine, and *Ski Utah*, *Lonely Planet*), thank you. The work these publications and boosters do to highlight and curate the best of life here elevates everybody's game and contributes to the quality of life in Utah. It often goes unsung but a strong, well-voiced media that is both chiding, cheeky and supportive makes things better for all. Support your local magazines!

Also thanks to Stuart Graves who is simply the most enthusiastic Salt Laker possible and Jennifer Bigler who has lugged books, set up events and built some very intense spreadsheets to keep this book up to speed. Finally, thanks for the baristas at Coffee Noir (1035 E. 200 S, Salt Lake City, UT 84102) who kept me fueled with caffeine and chill music.

● ●

©Matt Crawley

FOOD AND DRINK

GET DINNER FIXINGS
AT THE DOWNTOWN FARMERS MARKET

The Downtown Farmers Market is a social occasion and a weekly Saturday morning ritual for most Salt Lakers (and their dogs). Try not to forget that actual farmers are there selling gorgeous fruits, vegetables, and more. You'll also find producers of cheese, local meats, a juried selection of crafts, and booths filled with yummy immigrant cuisines. Carefully curated, everything at the market is locally grown and made. Go early to beat the crowds, and pick up fresh produce, a loaf of bread, and a wedge of cheese, and invite all the friends you saw at the market over for Saturday night dinner.

Downtown Farmers Market
June through October
Historic Pioneer Park, 300 S 300 W, Salt Lake City, 801-328-5070
slcfarmersmarket.org

OTHER FARMERS MARKETS AROUND THE VALLEY

Murray Farmers Market at Murray City Park
July through October
200 E 5200 S, Murray
murray.utah.gov

Wasatch Front Farmers Market at Gardner Village
Saturdays, July through October
1100 W 7800 S, West Jordan
wasatchfrontfarmersmarket.org

Sugar House Farmers Market at Fairmont Park
June through October
1040 E Sugarmont Drive, Salt Lake City

Wasatch Front Farmers Market at Wheeler Farm
June through October
6351 S 900 E, Salt Lake City
wasatchfrontfarmersmarket.org

BAR HOP
ON "WHISKEY STREET"

In Salt Lake City's frontier days, a section of Main Street was dubbed "Whiskey Street" by both Mormon teetotalers and whiskey-loving gentiles. (Note: early LDS Church members called nonbelievers by this culturally appropriated term.) This section of town, and the area around, were where a feller could go for a tipple if it suited him. Now, Whiskey Street is back—in a sense.

In 2009, the Salt Lake City Council loosened an ordinance that limited bars to just two for each of SLC's very long blocks. Soon— gasp—there were two, three, four, five, and then more bars all in a row. The first to test the relaxed waters was Bar X and Beer Bar on nearby 200 South. But then a bar actually named Whiskey Street opened on lower Main Street, a few doors from Cheers to You. Once the only bar on the block, Cheers to You is still a classic SLC dive. More bars followed, reviving the Whiskey Street of yore.

But these aren't the rough-and-tumble, sawdust-on-the-floor joints of the past; they draw mostly the younger, hipper, and flush-with-expense-account-cash set. Boasting deep liquor libraries, craft cocktails and beer, and upscale food, the bars on Whiskey Street are a hopping spot to crawl on a weekend night.

White Horse Spirits & Kitchen

One of the quieter spots on lower Main Street, White Horse prides itself on its selection of aperitifs and yummy menu of bar bites featuring locally sourced fare.

325 Main St., Salt Lake City, 801-363-0137
whitehorseslc.com

Whiskey Street

This hopping spot, specializing in hard-to-find whiskeys and other spirits, has a very tall, very impressive wall of booze that's serviced by a library ladder. I sure do wish, though, they'd get rid of the big TVs blocking all those beautiful bottles.

323 S Main St., Salt Lake City, 801-433-1371

whiskeystreet.com

Cheers to You

Always a classic, with cheap drinks, bowling trophies behind the bar, and a semi-surly bunch of regulars. Oh, and karaoke.

315 S Main St., Salt Lake City, 801-575-6400

Alibi Bar & Place

Alibi has a tight bar crew, excellent cocktails, and walls of art by local artists Dan Cassaro and Dan Christofferson of Beeteeth Studios (store.beeteeth.com), who share a whimsical affinity for Masonic-themed creations.

369 S Main St., Salt Lake City

Instagram: @alibislc

Maxwells

This SLC offshoot of a Park City local's fave is a big, big space surrounding a great horseshoe bar. Afternoons and early evenings, it's a great place to watch a sportsball match; later, it turns clubby. No matter what time, they serve up great pizza, by the slice even.

357 S Main St., Salt Lake City, 801-328-0304

maxwellssaltlakecity.com

Quarters

Hankering to drink and play Pac-Man? This twenty-one-and-older arcade bar has a full slate of retro and modern video games, pinball machines, and video-game-themed cocktails. Bring along your screen-addled friends.

5 E 400 S, Salt Lake City

quartersslc.com

TAKE A MAGICAL MYSTERY TOUR
(OF SUSHI)

Dinner at Takashi is a no-reservations affair; you'll wait your turn like every other hungry sushi aficionado. But boy is it worth the wait! The fish is as fresh as you'll find at four thousand feet above sea level (flown in daily), and you'll find Takashi Gibo behind the sushi bar most nights of the week. Beautiful cuts of sashimi are a must as is a tour of the kitchen menu (don't miss the aptly named "Ridiculously Tender Flank Steak"), but Takashi's inventive and sublime rolls are the main event. Creative concoctions such as "Strawberry Fields" and the "Sgt. Pepper" (Gibo is a big Beatles fan) are subtly done and contrast with the overdone rolls cluttering the American sushi landscape. Also try the "T & T" roll and its accompanying "Hotter Than Hell" sauce, which is as advertised.

Takashi, 18 W Market St., Salt Lake City, 801-519-9595
takashisushi.com

TIP

Takashi Gibo and his wife, Tamara, recently opened Post Office Place, a beautifully appointed cocktail spot next door to his Salt Lake sushi spot. The bar gets its name from its location in the old Salt Lake City Post Office building and is a great spot to wait for your table next door (which is a thing). Post Office Place serves PeruvianAsian fusion cocktails, small plates, and bar bites (the mashup works, trust me) to stave of your hunger in anticipation of Takashi's masterful sushi preparations.

Post Office Place, 16 W. Market St., Salt Lake City, 801-519-9595

EAT AT THE HOME
OF "KILLER MEXICAN FOOD"

The world-famous home of "Killer Mexican Food," Red Iguana, lives up to the hype. The hot spot run by the Cardenas family serves up Oaxacan cuisine in a wild environment, lined with punky bric-a-brac. The late, great Ramon Cardenas was a lover of music, and the walls feature signatures and autographed shrines to Carlos Santana, Los Lobos, ZZ Top, and Alejandro, to name just a few. Red Iguana is still a stop for rock 'n' rollers passing through. (Lady Gaga once famously ordered ninety tacos for her crew as takeout on the way out of town.) And the food is yum. Red Iguana has the requisite burritos, tacos, and enchiladas. But venture further on the massive menu, and you'll find authentic Mexican soups, delicious meat preparations, and a selection of moles made the hard way, every day, by Red Iguana's dedicated crew.

Red Iguana, 736 W North Temple, Salt Lake City, 801-322-1489
Red Iguana 2, 866 W South Temple, Salt Lake City, 801-214-6050
rediguana.com

TIP
The restaurant's second location, just one block from the original, is often less crowded.

SKI IN
FOR A WHISKEY TASTING

When David Perkins was looking around for a place to begin his career as a distiller of fine whiskey, Utah was not first on his list. Not only did our famously teetotaling state not have any distilleries, but there was also some question as to whether it was even allowed under Utah law. So he dusted off the Utah Code and found that distilleries were not only allowed, but had also been a major part of Utah history. The settling Mormons had sold whiskey to wagon parties headed through the territory en route to the West Coast. In 2009, Perkins applied for and received the first license to distill spirits in Utah since the 1870s. Now his award-winning, small-batch ryes and bourbons are prized bottles in the whiskey world, and High West can boast the world's only ski-in, ski-out whiskey-tasting room at the bottom of Park City's Town Lift (which also has a package store, open on Sundays). Also, liquor stores, even in unUtah Park City, are closed on Sunday. But High West has a package store that sells its spirits seven days a week.

High West Distillery and Saloon, 703 Park Ave., Park City, 435-649-8300
highwest.com

TIP
High West offers tours and tastings at its distillery in Wanship. The booze-making operation is located at Blue Sky Utah, a beautiful facility that also hosts weddings and other events.

27649 Old Lincoln Hwy., Wanship, 435-252-0662
blueskyutah.com

HOIST A TANKARD
AT BEER BAR

A sister to her swankier neighbor Bar X, Beer Bar is a rowdier affair. Long picnic tables in the style of a German beer garden stripe the wide room. Behind the bar you'll find a crew that takes its beer seriously, serving a pilsner in a pilsner glass, a lager in a lager glass, and, well, you get the idea. With a rotating cast of draughts on tap and an even more impressive selection of bottled brews from around Utah, the United States, and the world, Beer Bar is Salt Lake's finest spot to quaff a stein. Cut the alcohol with a daring selection from local butcher/ magician Frody Volgger's cured meat preparations, from traditional wurst to the delicious chicken and apple sausage.

Beer Bar, 161 E 200 S, Salt Lake City, 385-259-0905
beerbarslc.com

TIP

Next door to Beer Bar is Bar X, once a dive bar that infamously refused to serve women until the late 1980s. In 2011, however, new owners (including actor Ty Burrell, who plays Phil Dumphy on TVs *Modern Family*) arrived and turned the dank watering hole into, well, an "upscale" dank watering hole. Now, meticulously crafted cocktails are served with painstaking care in a speakeasy-style lounge.

Bar X, 155 E 200 S, Salt Lake City
barxsaltlake.com

QUAFF A CRAFT BEER
(AND UNDERSTAND THE FINE PRINT)

Craft beer in Utah comes with an asterisk, owing to unique liquor laws: beer that contains 4 percent alcohol by volume (or 3.2 percent by weight—it's confusing, we know) can be sold in grocery stores and on tap. Higher-alcohol brews are all bottled or canned and must be sold at liquor stores and at bars and restaurants. What does all this mean? Better brews. See, Utah beer makers brew a wide range of top-notch craft beers at all alcohol levels and routinely win big at the Great American Beer Festival. That said, the two-tiered system means our brewmasters can't just cover up mistakes by pumping up the alcohol content when they brew at 4 percent for taps and grocery store sales. Basically, making a craft beer in Utah requires more craft.

UTAH'S BEST BREWERIES AND BREWPUBS
Epic Brewery

Specializing in high-point beers, Epic's tasting room on State Street also includes a package store selling cold beer (the beer sections in liquor stores aren't refrigerated, so this is a bonus).

What to try: Spiral Jetty IPA

825 S State St., Salt Lake City, 801-906-0123

epicbrewing.com

Utah Brewers Cooperative (Squatters and Wasatch)

The two granddaddies of Utah brewing banded together a few years back to distribute their popular beers. The cheeky Greg Schirf, who once famously dressed like an early American colonist and dumped kegs of beer into the

Great Salt Lake to protest high alcohol taxes, founded Wasatch. Squatters, by contrast, is a more staid but still solid brand. Both make great beer that's easily found on tap handles and in stores around the state.

What to try (Squatters): Full Suspension Pale Ale

What to try (Wasatch): Polygamy Porter

1762 S 300 W, Salt Lake City, 801-466-8855

utahbeers.com

Bonneville Brewery

An upstart located near the shores of the Great Salt Lake, Bonneville's mad-scientist brewer, Dave Watson, makes a lovely range of beers from his brewery in the western wilderness. You'll find his work on tap handles at the All-Star bowling chain (the brewery's owner) or after a worth-it drive out to their brewery and restaurant in Tooele.

What to try: Antelope Amber Ale

1641 N Main St., Tooele, 435-248-0646

bonnevillebrewery.com

Fisher Brewing

Fisher Brewing was one of Utah's early breweries, opening in Salt Lake City in 1884. The brewery was founded by a German immigrant, Albert Fisher. The brewery survived Prohibition but shuttered in 1957. Fisher's great-great-grandson revived the family label and opened a brewery and tasting room in Salt Lake's up-and-coming Granary District.

What to try: the original Fisher Lager, sold in giant to-go cans if you want to bring some home.

320 W 800 S, Salt Lake City, 801-487-2337

fisherbeer.com

Proper Brewing Company

Also in the growing Granary District is Proper Brewing. The tasting room is also a game room, with shuffleboard, skee ball, and other bar games. Get a burger at Proper Burger, right next door.

What to try: Ziggy IPA, a fruity high-point beer that packs a punch

857 Main St., Salt Lake City, 801-953-1707

theproperbrewing.com

WALK INTO THE WOODS
FOR A DINING ADVENTURE

You'll bundle up at Solitude Mountain Resort's base area, strap on snowshoes, and take a walk through the snowy woods as the last sun of the day dwindles to twilight. At the end of the path lies the snow-covered Solitude Yurt. Shake off the snow, hang your coat, and wrap your fingers around the hot toddy that greets your arrival. It's time to dine.

The one-seating-a-night experience is a feast in all the appropriate ways. A parade of chef-chosen delights comes from the rickety kitchen for creation in full view of your communal table. The wine flows, and strangers become friends in the warm confines of the round Mongolian-style yurt. For your stumble back to reality, headlamps and a friendly guide lead the way to bed and the promise of another day on the mountain.

Solitude Yurt, 12000 Big Cottonwood Canyon, Entry 2, Solitude, 801-534-1400
solitudemountain.com

SAVOR
RUBY SNAP COOKIES

A recent finalist in *Salt Lake* magazine's "Best Chocolate-Chip Cookie in Utah" competition, Trudy, a classic chocolate-chip cookie, is just one of the delicious fresh cookies behind the counter at Ruby Snap's retro-chic shop on Salt Lake's west side.

Ruby Snap's original name was Dough Girl. But that moniker poked the belly of a certain Dough Boy, whose lawyers sent some very ungiggly cease-and-desist letters to the little Utah cookie shop. After a brief legal skirmish, the shop opted for Ruby Snap instead of Dough Girl and kept on turning out mouth-watering delights.

All the cookies are named after pin-up girls from the 1940s. My favorite? The Judy, a velvety orange dough full of citrus zest, topped with a buttery cream-cheese frosting. My grandmother used to make cookies just like this, and every bite transports me back to my childhood.

Ruby Snap, 770 S 300 W, Salt Lake City, 801-834-6111
rubysnap.com

EAT FUNERAL POTATOES
AT THE GARAGE ON BECK

Funeral potatoes are another Utah inside joke. The cheesy, casserole-style potatoes are often served at funerals and other large church and family gatherings, but the gooey, calorie-heavy tubers, often topped with crunchy corn flakes or potato chips, are downright delicious. The roadhouse bar, Garage on Beck, has fun with the local fare by frying them up into croquette-ish bites. Additionally, the Garage is one of the best spots for live music, and enjoying Sunday brunch on its friendly backyard-style patio is not to be missed. Also try grandma's pot pie.

Garage on Beck, 1199 Beck St., Salt Lake City, 801-521-3904
garageonbeck.com

EAT THE BEST LOBSTER ROLL
IN THE WORLD—OR IN UTAH

It was a brave person who, no doubt driven by intense hunger, was the first to eat a lobster. Even more fearless were New Englanders Ben and Lorin Smaha, who brought fresh lobster to Utah.

The Smahas grew up in New England, Ben in Cape Elizabeth, Maine, and Lorin in Lebanon, New Hampshire. The two East Coasters boasted that they could have fresh whole lobster to your party "from shore to door in 24"—hours, that is. They started Freshies Lobster Company as a catering operation in Park City in 2009, in a nod to ski slang for fresh powder snow. Then they opened a store front in Park City in 2014 and a second in Salt Lake City in 2018. That same year, *Down East* magazine named the lobster roll from Freshies "The World's Best Lobster Roll." And with a name like *Down East* magazine, they must know, right?

Hands down, they're the best lobster rolls I've had since my last trip to Maine. Served in a buttered and toasted top-slit bun, they have little besides lobster—which is the point. Discernible claw and tail meat chunks overflow the bun. Served simply with kettle chips, the Real Maine-ah roll with its 3.7 ounces of lobster meat isn't enough. So be sure to order the XL.

Park City
1897 Prospector Ave., Park City
435-631-9861
freshieslobsterco.com

Salt Lake City
356 E 900 S, Salt Lake City
801-829-1032
freshieslobsterco.com

YODEL ALONG
AT SNOWBIRD'S OKTOBERFEST

The annual Oktoberfest at Snowbird Resort is a great chance to get up into the mountains before the snow flies. Starting in September, owing to the cooling temperatures in the high-mountain setting, the festival features the requisite oom-pah-pah bands, lederhosen, and, of course, beer.

Snowbird's summertime activities, zip lines, alpine slide, and mountain coaster are open for business as is the iconic Snowbird Tram. It's a nice way to wind summer down, sit in the sun, and hoist a stein, eat a bratwurst, and shop the trinkets in the vendors' area.

Snowbird Center, 9385 S Snowbird Center Dr., Snowbird, 801-933-2222
snowbird.com/events/oktoberfest

TIP

The local brand of mountain wear, Kühl clothing, always brings a selection of clearance items for sale at Oktoberfest. The high-quality technical clothing is let go for fire-sale prices at the clothier's booth.

kuhl.com

WOLF DOWN
A PASTRAMI BURGER
AT CROWN BURGER

Crown Burger is a local chain of chargrilled burgers and home to the pastrami burger, a quarter-pounder topped with a wad of smoky meat. Meat on meat, if you will. Several copycats can be found in SLC, but the original is the best.

Although famed LA food critic Jonathan Gold traces the concoction's origin to Southern California, it has taken root here in Utah. This is the burger expat Utahns hunger for.

Crown Burger, 377 E 200 S, Salt Lake City, 801-532-1155
crown-burgers.com

Other pastrami burger joints:

Apollo Burger, 950 W 1700 S, Salt Lake City, 801-532-4301
apolloburgers.com
B&D Burger, 222 S 1300 E, Salt Lake City, 801-582-7200
banddburgers.com
Greek Souvlaki, 404 E 300 S, Salt Lake City, 801-322-2062
greeksouvlaki.com

ORDER UP
SOME LION HOUSE ROLLS

The Lion House was occupied by Salt Lake's founder and perhaps most famous resident, Brigham Young. Located on the LDS Church Headquarters grounds, adjacent to another of Brigham's stately homes (the Beehive House), the Lion House is a reception hall and restaurant. The warm, fluffy rolls—traditionally part of many Salt Lakers' Thanksgiving celebrations—are its signature menu item, and a walk by the place in the morning as the rolls bake inside will have your stomach growling. The Lion House Pantry is open daily except Sunday.

Lion House Pantry, 63 E South Temple, Salt Lake City, 801-539-3616
templesquare.com/lion-house

CHASE DOWN
A FOOD TRUCK

Salt Lake's weekly gathering of food trucks at Gallivan Plaza is a central space for sampling the very best of SLC's food truck fare, from 11 a.m. to 2 p.m. on Thursdays. You can also check out Roaminghunger.com/slc to locate the food truck near you and follow your favorites on Twitter and Facebook to get daily updates on where they'll be parked each day.

Another truck assembly occurs at Soho Food Park, which gathers regulars Monday through Saturday for lunch and dinner. There are heaters in the winter, umbrellas in the summer, and tables. Follow @sohofoodpark on Twitter to get a daily lineup and plan your lunch break.

Food Truck Thursdays, 11 a.m.–2 p.m.
Gallivan Center, 239 S Main St., Salt Lake City
thegallivancenter.com

Soho Food Park, 4747 S Holladay Blvd., Holladay
Roaminghunger.com/slc
facebook.com/sohofoodpark

FAVORITE FOOD TRUCKS

Cup Bop, Korean BBQ
facebook.com/Cupbop

Waffle Love, Belgian waffles
waffluv.com

Kotako, Korean tacos
facebook.com/kotakotruck

Fat Kid Mac 'n' Cheese, decadent mac and cheese
fatkidmacncheese.com

Chop City, an all-pork, all-pork-serving food truck. Yes!
facebook.com/chopcityslc

EAT A BRIGHAM CITY PEACH
ON FRUIT WAY

Take a drive north on I-15, get off the freeway at the Willard exit, and get on Utah Highway 89. This is the southern tip of the famed "Fruit Way," where you'll discover roadside produce stands featuring the best of the state's growing season, including the luscious Brigham City peach. The famous peaches are celebrated every year in September during the northern town's annual Peach Days Festival. Although the beautiful peaches are sort of the star of Utah's produce pantheon, many fruit and vegetable festivals can be found around the state that offer pleasant helpings of small-town charm and low-rent pageantry to celebrate the cornucopia of Utah's growing season.

FRUIT AND VEGETABLES FESTIVALS

JUNE

Strawberry Days, Pleasant Grove
strawberrydays.org

AUGUST

Bear Lake Raspberry Days, Garden City
gardencityut.us

Corn Festival, Enterprise
enterprisecornfest.wix.com/enterprisecornfest

Trout and Berry Days, Paradise
paradise.utah.gov

SEPTEMBER

Golden Onion Days, Payson
paysonutah.org

Peach Days, Brigham City
peachdays.org

Melon Days, Green River
melon-days.com

OCTOBER

Apple Fest, New Harmony
newharmonyfire.com

BRUNCH CREEK-SIDE
AT RUTH'S DINER

Ruth's Diner, opened in 1930, and is a classic roadside diner with a lovely and bucolic patio on the bank of Emigration Creek that draws the brunch crowd in droves every weekend. Ruth was a tough old broad known for not looking at IDs too hard. "They can enforce their own laws," she once said, and until she sold the restaurant in 1977, it had a smoking section (which is to say, wherever Ruth was smoking). She lived behind the restaurant until she passed away in 1989 at the age of 94, but her legend lives on. Don't miss the mile-high biscuits and the famous chocolate pudding.

Ruth's Diner, 4160 Emigration Canyon Rd., Salt Lake City, 801-582-5807
ruthsdiner.com

YOU WANT FRY SAUCE WITH THAT?
YES. YES, YOU DO.

In Utah, the acquisition of fries comes with a question: You want fry sauce with that? To the uninitiated, the question is befuddling. What is this fry sauce? Well, it's basically ketchup and mayonnaise, sometimes with a mystery ingredient (often relish and cayenne pepper), whirled together into a creamy, pink concoction. The ketchup-to-mayo ratio varies from establishment to establishment, and the particular calibration of the mix is a matter of individual taste.

It's hard to say who has the best fry sauce; it is, after all, a pretty simple condiment. But I've found that Hires Big H serves up an excellent emblematic cupful. Some folks in fancy places try to sneak it onto your plate by calling it "aioli," but we know. Dude, that's just fry sauce in a ramekin.

Hires Big H, 425 S 700 E, Salt Lake City, 801-364-4582
hiresbigh.com

Another place to try the fry sauce:
Crown Burger, 377 E 200 S, Salt Lake City, 801-532-1155
crown-burgers.com

EAT A FAMOUS PASTRY
AT LES MADELEINES

Pastry chef Romina Rasmussen created a national food sensation when she started making kouign amann at her shop Les Madeleines more than a decade ago. The kouign amann is a flaky, sweet, savory pastry from the Brittany region of France, but the labor-intensive and butter-rich pastry wasn't done much even in Parisian bakeries. Romina perfected her recipe and reintroduced the gooey delicacy to our mouths, even though we still can't pronounce it right. Her efforts have brought national attention from such renowned publications as *Food and Wine* and *Bon Appétit*, and she has been featured on the Food Network's *The Best Thing I Ever Ate.* Her shop is one of Salt Lake's favorite lunch stops, serving beautifully crafted sandwiches, salads, and pastries in tranquilly civilized surroundings. Stop in for lunch and walk out with a kouign amann for dessert.

Les Madeleines, 216 E 500 S, Salt Lake City, 801-355-2294
lesmadeleines.com

DRINK THE PERFECT
CUP OF COFFEE

Fastidious isn't a strong enough word to describe the owner of Caffe d'Bolla. John Piquet is a *nut* for his coffee and is nationally known as a roasting and brewing expert. He positively fusses over every cup he serves.

If you really want to see him in action, order a $12 cup of siphon coffee. It's an impressive procedure as he painstakingly fires up the siphon and serves you what may be the perfect cup of coffee. But don't ask for cream or sugar unless you want to see John's eyes roll completely out of his head and then be chased out of his coffee shop.

Caffe d'Bolla, 249 E 400 S, Salt Lake City, 801-355-1398
caffedbolla.com

GET A FROSTY
ROOT BEER AND A BURGER

Once upon a time, Hires Big H was part of a chain started by Hires Root Beer Company, and this last bastion of the empire is still serving amazing burgers after all these years, with a frosted mug of root beer on the side, naturally. Hires's founder, Don Hale, was a local Zig Ziglar of sorts, full of folksy wisdom, and you'll find his quotable witticisms around the restaurant and can even buy a book of his advice on your way out. The joint still has carhop service and sells the "secret recipe" root-beer base so you can make your own at home.

Hires Big H, 425 S 700 E, Salt Lake City, 801-355-1398
hiresbigh.com

GO TO MADDOX
ON THE WAY TO
GRANDMOTHER'S HOUSE

Located about an hour north of Salt Lake in Perry, Maddox Ranch House is one of those don't-miss-it, worth-the-drive restaurants. Still studded in the original 1950s steak house kitsch, Maddox remains family run and is still serving families on their way to grandmother's house.

The big neon sign outside boasts famous chicken, but actually it's sort of strange chicken, fried in a breading that some folks love and others, meh. Where this strange chicken-fried fry batter works best is on Maddox's chicken-fried steak. The thin breading covers a patty of ground sirloin that makes it one of the menu's biggest highlights. The steaks all come from grass-fed, free-range, etc., cattle that until just a decade or so ago would graze right outside the panoramic windows. The Ranch House also has a helping of bison steaks on the menu.

Every meal comes with all the trimmings, delicious rolls (with fresh-whipped raspberry honey butter), salad or seafood cocktail, and your choice of potato on the side, as is tradition. The pies are to die for, and the birch root beer brewed on-site by Irv Maddox, grandson of founder Irvin Maddox, is worth the sugary calories.

Maddox Fine Food, 1900 S Highway 89, Perry, 800-544-5474
maddoxfinefood.com

PUB CRAWL
ON SLC GREENBIKES

Salt Lake's GREENbikes follow the mold of bike-share programs in Austin, Texas, and New York City: you check out a bike, ride to a station near your destination, and drop the bike off. It's also a great way to crisscross the city and visit bars. The GREENbike pub crawl on the next page will take you from station to station in a nice, big loop around town. Always bike safely, wear a helmet, and dress appropriately. And if you get too blotto, please call an Uber, Lyft, or taxi.

GREENbikes
greenbikeslc.org

PUB CRAWL

STOP 1

Squatters Pub and Brewery
Bike station: Squatters Station
147 W Broadway, Salt Lake City

STOP 2

Twist Bar
Bike station: Rocky Mountain Power Station
225 S Main St., Salt Lake City

STOP 3

Copper Common
Bike station: TravelWise Station
160 E 300 S, Salt Lake City

STOP 4

Dick 'n' Dixies
300 S 300 E, Salt Lake City

STOP 5

Beer Bar and Bar X
Bike station: SLUG Mag Station
200 S 200 E, Salt Lake City

STOP 6

Beer Hive
Bike station: Energy Development Station
136 S Main St., Salt Lake City

REEK OF GARLIC

Cotton Bottom Inn is a great dive at the mouth of Big Cottonwood Canyon. In summer, the patio is filled with leather-clad bikers; in the winter, booted skiers and boarders crowd in after the lifts close each day. Its famous garlic burger is a strange creature served on a doughy hoagie roll, featuring American cheese with four garlic-powder-soaked patties, pickles, and a pepperoncini on the side. Everybody in your party will reek of garlic for the rest of the day, so you're all in this together.

Cotton Bottom Inn, 2820 E 6200 S, Salt Lake City, 801-273-9830
cottonbottominn.com

GET YOUR CHICKEN HOT
AT PRETTY BIRD

Viet Pham is perhaps Utah's most famous chef. His win over Bobby Flay in a challenge on *Iron Chef America* is the stuff of foodie lore here in Salt Lake City. But Forage, Pham's amazing restaurant, had already put Pham on the map.

Forage was an experience, a multicourse meal with whiz-bang molecular tastes and creative bites inspired by Pham's Malaysian heritage. But like many artists, Pham got bored with Forage and shuttered his world-renowned restaurant. After roaming the earth for new ideas, he finally returned from hiatus to thunder back into Utah's food pantheon.

His new concept, Pretty Bird, is the opposite of Forage. There are just two items on the menu: a fried-chicken sandwich and a chicken quarter. Pham has brought the famed Nashville hot chicken style to SLC—and yes, it is hot. Order the spiciest variant only if you're very brave. The small, lunch-counter-style spot behind the Eccles Theater draws the lunch crowd with long lines, and they often run out of chicken. So get there when the doors open.

Pretty Bird, 146 Regent St., Salt Lake City
prettybirdchicken.com

GO TO
HELL('S BACKBONE)
IN BOULDER

This book is pretty Salt Lake-centric. But Utah is a big place and when we talk about great food, we'd be remiss if we didn't direct you to Hell's Backbone Grill & Farm in Boulder, Utah. It's more than an award-winning restaurant and organic farm. Its story is inextricably tied to the fight for public lands in Utah. Founded in 1999 by Blake Spalding and Jen Castle, the restaurant and farm sit on the border of Grand-Staircase Escalante National Monument and were named for an imposing geographic landmark within the monument. The monument, created in 1996 by President Bill Clinton, is now under threat from anti-public land forces in Washington, D.C. Blake and Jen are outspoken advocates for the national monument, and their mission, as Blake says, is to "make people fall in love with this place so they will know it's worth saving."

President Clinton may have designated Utah's Grand Staircase-Escalante a national monument, but Blake and Jen put it on the world's culinary map. Their restaurant, on the grounds of Boulder Mountain Lodge, has received kudos from the *New York Times*, the *Salt Lake Tribune*, the *Wall Street Journal*, *Sunset* magazine, *National Geographic*, and *Oprah*. And it has received multiple awards from *Salt Lake* magazine. But that's not all. The restaurant has one of the highest Zagat ratings in Utah, and its chef-owners were semifinalists for the James Beard Foundation's "Best Chef in the Southwest" award in both 2017 and 2018.

The restaurant—open seasonally from mid-March through November (reservations recommended)—follows Buddhist principles. In accordance with its commitment to sustainability, environmental ethics, and community responsibility, it serves organic, locally produced, regionally and seasonally appropriate cuisine, growing much of its produce on a six-acre farm. The fruit comes largely from Boulder's heirloom orchards, and the meat comes from local ranchers. As if that wasn't Dao enough, monks from Drepung Monastery in Tibet visit each season to help on the farm.

Hell's Backbone Grill & Farm, Boulder, Utah, 435-335-7464
hellsbackbonegrill.com

Open seasonally from mid-March through November.
Reservations recommended.

RELAX AT APRÈS SKI
AFTER YOU SKI

The tradition of an after-ski-day beverage is ensconced in Utah's ski and snowboard culture. Sometimes the thrill of spending a day in the high mountains, gliding on the greatest snow on earth is rivaled by that pleasant feeling of plopping down on a stool in a rowdy bar or cozying up by the fire in a fancy lodge and ordering a beer and a shot (or a preciously concocted cocktail) as the sun sets on the mountain.

Here are my favorites for each of the nine (nine!) resorts within an hour of Salt Lake City:

ALTA SKI AREA
Alta Peruvian Lodge Bar
Loud, rowdy, and fun, with colorful memorabilia from seventy-five-plus years of Alta history all over the walls.
Rustlers Lodge
A snifter of brandy will do at this cozy spot to warm yourself by a roaring fire.

SNOWBIRD
BYOB to the Tram Deck
Bask in the sun at this hub of activity at Snowbird. Locals bring up small backpacker-style propane stoves to mix up hot toddies after a day on the steeps.

BRIGHTON
Molly Greens

Inside this classic A-frame ski chalet, you'll find the best pile of nachos in Utah and a pint of Cutthroat Ale waiting for you.

SNOWBASIN AND POWDER MOUNTAIN
Shooting Star Saloon

Crowd into Utah's oldest watering hole, located in the valley below both resorts, for a pitcher of Coors and a Shooting Star burger.

SUNDANCE
The Owl Bar

Belly up and sip a shot of whiskey at the restored 1890s wooden bar. It was moved from the Rosewood Bar in Thermopolis, Wyoming, to Sundance, Utah. The Rosewood was frequented by Butch Cassidy's Hole in the Wall Gang.

SOLITUDE
The Thirsty Squirrel

Order a brew and sprawl out at this comfy lounge in Solitude Village, a local favorite.

PARK CITY MOUNTAIN
The Corner Store Pub & Grill

Propane heaters warm a convivial and rowdy patio scene featuring $1 PBRs and hot wings.

DEER VALLEY
The St. Regis Bar and Lounge

Enjoy the famous Bloody Mary or a glass of fine wine around the fire pit on the patio.

MUSIC AND ENTERTAINMENT

TAKE THE TRAIN
FOR OGDEN TWILIGHT

Salt Lake City's humongous Twilight Concert Series foundered a few years ago. The popular, once-free shows got too big, and the series collapsed under the weight of its own success. With SLC's Twilight under transition (a new, more modest series replaced it in 2018), Utah's second city, Ogden, rushed in to fill the vacuum.

The Ogden Twilight series, like Ogden, is awesome. The smaller-sized shows with a younger concert lineup are held in a lovely amphitheater on Ogden's famed 25th Street. In the prohibition era, infamous gangster Al Capone once dubbed this row of bars and restaurants "Two Bit Street," opining that a fella could get anything he wanted for a quarter there. Ogden wears that rough-and-tumble past with pride and generally flaunts Utah's squeaky clean reputation.

Featured bands like Sylvan Esso and the Flaming Lips draw music-hungry Salt Lakers north to Ogden via the FrontRunner Train. The concert venue is just a short walk up 25th Street from the station.

43 E 25th Street, Ogden, 801-629-8000
ogdentwilight.com

TIP

Ogden Twilight tickets (only $10 in advance; $15 day of show) are also your ticket to ride the FrontRunner for free. Skip the traffic and take the train, go early, and cruise around 25th Street before the show. But be sure to watch the clock after the concert. The last train for Salt Lake leaves at 11:30 p.m.

SEE A SHOW
AT URBAN LOUNGE

This small, not-a-bad-spot-in-the-house music club is the place to see bands in Salt Lake on the way up the ladder of fame and stardom. The spartan club with cheap beer presents an eclectic lineup of acts, from twee indie bands to death-metal wizards and hip-hop kings pretty much seven nights a week. Urban Lounge shows start late, and the bands that play there inevitably return to play the small, informal space that lets you get right up front.

Urban Lounge, 241 S 500 E, Salt Lake City, 801-746-0557
theurbanloungeslc.com

TIP

Urban's owners Will and Mike Sartain know the punk rock vibe of Urban Lounge isn't for everyone. They recently opened a more civilized spot on Salt Lake's west edge called Metro Music Hall. The underground nightclub draws an eclectic mix of live bands and DJs and hosts drag, burlesque, and cabernet shows weekly.

615 W 100 S, Salt Lake City, 385-528-0952
metromusichall.com

BONUS TIP

The club owns the restaurant next door, Rye. Stop in for a preshow meal of hipster comfort food, yummy ramen, Asian-fusion fare, and craft cocktails. During shows, the restaurant reveals televisions with cameras on the stage next door and pipes in the sound.

PICNIC IT UP
AT A RED BUTTE SHOW

This wonderful amphitheater situated in the eastern foothills of the Salt Lake Valley is the setting for a signature Salt Lake moment: a great concert in a great setting. There isn't a bad seat in the house, and a liberal picnic policy that allows your own food and drink makes this a social scene. In fact, there's a whole culture of folks who get up there early and wait for the gates to open at 6 p.m. to rush in and throw down the blankets. Red Butte books excellent midrange acts, such as David Byrne, Alabama Shakes, and Jason Isbell. The concerts, which run from May into September, often sell out. Beyond the amphitheater is the beautiful Red Butte Garden, a large botanical garden for strolling through before and during the show.

Red Butte Garden, 300 Wakara Way, Salt Lake City, 801-585-0556
redbuttegarden.org/concerts

TIP

Red Butte Garden members get first crack at ticket sales when the season is announced plus free garden admissions and other perks. The reasonable membership fee helps support education and outreach efforts at the garden.

TOUR THE CITY
ON ELECTRIC WHEELS

One day they weren't here. The next they were. Like many other US cities, Salt Lake got scootered. Stand-up electric-powered scooters started showing up around town in the summer of 2018, catching city leaders flat-footed and grumbling about all the kids zooming around. But despite continued fist-shaking by many older folk, the zooming seems here to stay.

The two companies (at press time; there are rumors of more), Bird and Lime, check out their zippy rides via app, much like you'd call a Lyft or an Uber ride. They're cheap ($1 to check out and 15 cents a mile), plentiful, and, yeah, yeah, fun. They're most plentiful in downtown Salt Lake City even though Bird and Lime have placated city leaders with promises of serving transit-starved neighborhoods outside the city core. Final finger-wagging aside, you can grab one and take it around the city to see the sites or stop in restaurants, shops, and bars and just leave the darn thing anywhere. You whippersnappers just stay off the sidewalks!

Lime
li.me

Bird
bird.co

SEE A SHOW
AT KILBY COURT

This all-ages venue is an SLC institution. An entire generation of disenfranchised Salt Lake youth found themselves at Kilby and along the way witnessed the growth of the Salt Lake indie scene. Many major bands have passed through the Court on their way up the indie music ladder (Iron and Wine, Deathcab for Cutie, Neon Trees, Fall Out Boy), and the small space, hidden down an alley on Salt Lake's west side, remains a place for youngsters to discover great new music and be a part of something larger than homework and high school. Don't worry. It's not just for kids (although they are there). It's truly a unique spot to hear music.

Kilby Court, 741 S Kilby Court, Salt Lake City, 800-513-7540
kilbycourt.com

TUNE IN TO THE SOUNDTRACK OF LIFE
IN SALT LAKE

The beloved community radio station KRCL, with its eclectic mix of music and progressive community involvement, is the constant backbeat to life in Salt Lake. It's playing in our cars, our workplaces, and around our houses—pretty much constantly. Take, for example, a typical chore-filled Saturday. The day opens up with coffee and Shannalee's *Saturday Breakfast Jam*, followed by Grateful Dead–laced deep tracks on Dave Santivasi's *Saturday Sagebrush Serenade* (including a meditation for world peace every week at noon). The day moves along with Courtney's *Afternoon Delight,* a quirky three-hour mix of indie, new wave, old soul, and new rock. And you'll be putting away the tools while Robert Nelson's *Smile Jamaica* plays his trademark "all killer, no filler" three--hour block of reggae and dub music. Weekday mornings with John Florence (a not-so closeted Dead Head), lunchtime with the woman who rocks, Eugenie, and drive time with my fave Ebay Hamilton. In a world of boring commercial radio stations, homogeneous satellite radio, and computer algorithms programing our listening, KRCL offers a beautifully human blend of music and activism, and is an essential part of living the good life in Salt Lake.

KRCL 90.9 FM, 1971 W North Temple, Salt Lake City, 801-363-1818
krcl.org

SPEND THE DAY
AT LAGOON

The wooden roller coaster, known simply as "the roller coaster," is the foundation of an excellent un-themed amusement park thirty minutes north of Salt Lake. The rickety old coaster hearkens back to Lagoon's turn-of-the-century origins, but the modern park features all manner of whirligigs and geegaws to fling you and your crew every which way. The sprawling one-hundred-plus-acre park also includes a water park (bring your swimsuit), a zoo (accessed by a goofy train that runs around its namesake lagoon), and a Pioneer Village complete with authentic pioneer buildings and a daily shootout show at high noon.

Lagoon, 375 Lagoon Dr., Farmington, 801-451-8000
lagoonpark.com

VISIT THE STATE ROOM

Salt Lake's music scene got a shot in the arm in 2009 when longtime Red Butte promoter Chris Mautz and his partner Darin Picoli founded The State Room. The well-designed space is dedicated to its acoustically beloved sound stage. Inside the theater are no tawdry beer signs or anything really to distract from the stage, which is fronted by a roomy dance floor and backed by tiered seats for those who like to have a seat. The bar out front offers a civilized coat check, an efficient bar staff, and reasonably priced drinks. The State Room is open only for shows—a range of midlevel to big bands in a wonderfully intimate space that puts live music first.

The State Room, 638 S State St., Salt Lake City, 801-596-3560
thestateroom.com

TIP
Mautz and Picoli decided that, as awesome as The State Room is, they wanted a venue for bigger bands and bigger crowds. Behold The Commonwealth Room, The State Room on steroids. The format is exactly the same: decent bar prices, excellent sound, and even another giant disco ball.

195 2100 S, Salt Lake City, 801-741-4200
thecommonwealthroom.com

SEE THE STARS
AT THE CLARK PLANETARIUM

Space is cool, and the Clark Planetarium has plenty of it—three floors of exhibits for the little Neil Armstrong in all of us. Its heart and soul is the star-show planetarium called the Hansen Dome, a state-of-the-art, 360-degree projection system that goes way beyond the field-trip star shows of your childhood. (It also has, of course, the requisite late-night Laser Zeppelin and Floyd shows to help you recall your forgotten college years.) The Clark is also home to an IMAX theater showing blockbuster films in the biggest format on earth as well as more educational fare.

Clark Planetarium at the Gateway, 110 S 400 W, Salt Lake City, 385-468-7827
clarkplanetarium.org

GO TO THEATER
THAT'S NOT *IN* A THEATER

I enjoy plays, but if you've seen hundreds of productions in your lifetime like I have, they tend to blend together. So when I discovered Sackerson, a small guerrilla company in SLC, my love for theater was reignited. This teeny outfit, founded in 2014 by Dave Mortensen, Alex Ungerman, Daniel Whiting, and playwright Morag Shepherd, is creating and performing some of the most interesting theater in the state.

Take *Hindsight*, a production in summer 2018. The play was staged on the streets of Salt Lake City, although it most certainly is not "street theater." The small audience, limited to five for each performance, met at Temple Square and was given wireless headphones and told to follow. Yes, follow. The audience followed the actors, who wore microphones piped into the headphones. And we did follow, first onto a passing UTA bus, then down the street, into restaurants, and all round the city. And all the while, a quite beautiful play about young love unfolded, in reverse.

Hindsight, just one of Sackerson's innovative productions, was a sensation, selling out and adding a second season. Sackerson doesn't have a theater space or a stage, so visit the website and follow the company on Facebook to find out what they'll cook up next.

sackerson.org

TIP

For more than forty years, the Salt Lake Acting Company has been producing an annual send-up of Utah politics and LDS Church culture called *Saturday's Voyeur*. The campy production—filled with inside jokes; wacky plots; parodies of popular songs; and caricatures of local politicians, church leaders, and news-making figures—is a Utah classic.

Salt Lake Acting Company
168 W 500 N, Salt Lake City, 801-363-7522
saltlakeactingcompany.org

RENT *RUBIN AND ED*
AT TOWER THEATRE

Tower Theatre is the flagship of the Utah Film Society, a Sundance venue during the independent film festival, and where you'll find showings of all the foreign films, esoteric documentaries, period pieces, and Helen Mirren vehicles you'd ever want to see. The theater's lobby also has a collection of rare and hard-to-find DVDs that you won't find on Netflix or Amazon.

Do yourself a favor and rent *Rubin and Ed*, an out-of-print movie filmed in Utah in the early 1990s. Starring Crispin Glover and Howard Hesseman, the oddball buddy flick is about, umm, two guys going out to the desert to bury a frozen cat.

Tower Theatre, 876 E 900 S, Salt Lake City, 801-321-0310
saltlakefilmsociety.org

TIP
Another of the best movies about our city is the 1998 independent film *SLC Punk!* The charmingly funny, oddball picture follows the lives of two misfit punks in the 1980s. Make it a double feature.

"HALLELUJAH"
WITH THE UTAH SYMPHONY

Come Christmastime, the Utah Symphony performs Handel's *Messiah* for a glorious sing-along in Abravanel Hall. The jubilant event is one of the hot tickets of the holiday season. You know the chorus, right?

Abravanel Hall, 123 W South Temple, Salt Lake City, 801-533-6683
utahsymphony.org

TIP

The Utah Symphony also performs a popular outdoor concert series every summer at Deer Valley Ski Resort. The pops series plays the hits, including its popular performances of the *1812 Overture*, complete with cannon accompaniment. Bring your picnic and enjoy a civilized evening under the stars.

WATCH YOUR KID
(OR YOUR NEIGHBOR'S KID)
DANCE IN *THE NUTCRACKER*

Ballet West is one of the oldest ballet companies in America and continues to mount challenging works of ballet and modern dance. But every tiny dancer dreams of dancing with the Sugar Plum Fairy, right? Each year, thousands of aspiring young dancers audition for the right to play a part in the annual performances of *The Nutcracker* at Capitol Theatre, alongside company members and guest professionals. Ballet West also produces a satirical version of the famous ballet called *The Nutty Nutcracker*. The annual just-for-yucks production pulls its jokes from the previous year's collection of pop culture winners and losers (including, one year, making fun of Ballet West's inclusion in the reality show *Breaking Pointe*), and crams them into something loosely resembling a ballet.

Capitol Theatre, 50 E 200 S, Salt Lake City, 801-869-6900
balletwest.org

SEE A CONCERT
IN THE "SUPERNACLE"

The giant LDS Conference Center was built in 2000, primarily to host the Church of Jesus Christ of Latter-Day Saints's semiannual gatherings (called simply "conferences"); but many other musical and performance events are held there—namely, the free-but-hard-to-get-a-ticket-to Mormon Tabernacle Choir Christmas concerts. An engineering marvel with insanely fastidious acoustics, the 1.4-million-square-foot center seats twenty-one thousand people and is large enough to hold two imaginary Boeing 747s side by side. The view from every seat of the house is "miraculously" unobstructed by support pillars. You can also take a tour of the joint, including the beautiful rooftop gardens.

LDS Conference Center, 60 N Temple, Salt Lake City, 801-240-0075
lds.org/locations/temple-square-conference-center

SPORTS AND RECREATION

PADDLE OUTRIGGER CANOES
ON GREAT SALT LAKE

Utah is home to many Pacific Islanders, thanks to early missionary efforts by the LDS Church in the Polynesian islands. So very far from the idyllic shores of their homeland, a group of transplanted Hawaiians brought the traditional outrigger canoe to the waters of Great Salt Lake and founded Hui Paoakalani, a paddling club at GSL Marina. The club hosts the Annual Duke Paoa Kahanamoku Water Fest (Duke was an Olympic medal–winning swimmer) in June and goes out for paddle sessions from 10 a.m. to 3 p.m. every Saturday from April through mid-September.

Great Salt Lake Marina, 1075 S 13312 W, Magna
huipaoakalani.blogspot.com; gslmarina.com

DIVING IN THE DESERT?
SCUBA AT FIVE THOUSAND FEET ABOVE SEA LEVEL

Landlocked Utah isn't a place you'd think of for scuba diving, but we've got two of the world's most unique spots for underwater adventure—Bonneville Seabase and the Homestead Crater. Seabase is carved out of the salty earth above a natural warm mineral spring in Grantsville, Utah—quite literally, in the desert near the shores of Great Salt Lake. Seabase's main diving area, called Habitat Bay, is stocked with tropical fish and, yikes, sharks (friendly nurse sharks).

The Homestead Crater, located in Midway, is equally strange—a mineral water pool located inside a rocky caldera. In the 1990s, intrepid divers drilled into the rock to access the ninety-degree water inside and built a diving and snorkeling area. The warm, crystal-clear waters are an eerie blue, and divers can descend as far as sixty feet into the crater's depths.

Bonneville Seabase, 1600 UT-138, Grantsville, 435-884-3874
seabase.net

Homestead Crater, 700 Homestead Dr., Midway, 435-657-3840
homesteadresort.com

ONE MINUTE OF TERROR:
RIDE THE OLYMPIC BOBSLED TRACK

After I completed my one-minute blast down the official bobsled track of the 2002 Winter Olympics at Utah Olympic Park, I thought, "I'll never do that again." This is a true bucket-list item, such as skydiving or going to the top of the Empire State Building. Do it. Once. And if you can't muster the courage to sign the lengthy waiver, tamer activities are available at Utah Olympic Park. In the summertime, the park has zip lines, alpine slides (a mini-bobsled, if you will), summer tubing (yes, that's a thing), and its popular show featuring the athletes of the US freestyle ski aerials team flipping and flying into the pool they use for summer training.

Utah Olympic Park, 3419 Olympic Pkwy., Park City, 435-658-4200
utaholympiclegacy.org

HIKE TO THE "LIVING ROOM"
FOR SUNSET

In the foothills above the University of Utah, a spider's web of trails snakes up the hillside, a popular area used by trail runners, dog walkers, and mountain bikers. The Living Room hike will take you up to a set of rocks arranged like a sofa and chairs that Fred Flintstone would appreciate. If you make the hike for the sunset, remember to bring headlamps for the walk down in twilight.

Living Room Trailhead, 383 Colorow Rd., Salt Lake City

CHOOSE SIDES
IN THE "HOLY WAR"

Football rivalry takes on biblical proportions each year when the BYU Cougars meet the University of Utah Utes on the gridiron. The spirited rivalry between the LDS Church-owned private school and the state university brings up the division between Mormons and non-Mormons in an annual contest of vulgarity (Ute fans) and pious sneers (Cougar fans) that spills out across the city. The big game, for most, is a socially acceptable way for gentiles to fly their flags in the face of the dominant religion. The rivalry has diminished in importance since Utah joined the Pac-12 and BYU went the independent route in 2011, but its cultural significance remains.

Rice-Eccles Stadium, 451 S 1400 E, Salt Lake City, 801-581-8849
utahtickets.com

LaVell Edwards Stadium, 1700 North Canyon Rd., Provo, 801-422-2981
byutickets.com

TIP

The game alternates between Salt Lake City and Provo, but the festivities are somewhat diminished at Cougar Stadium. Catch the tailgate near the Utes' Rice-Eccles Stadium for the rowdiest display of Ute pride. But if you can't get a ticket to the big rivalry game, any game day at Rice-Eccles is a must-do event in Salt Lake City.

WALK AMONG THE WILDFLOWERS
AT ALTA IN ALBION BASIN

July is peak wildflower season in Utah, and one of the best spots to see this annual outbreak of beauty is Albion Basin above Alta Ski Resort. The wildflower bloom depends on the weather, but traditionally its peak occurs around July 24 (Pioneer Day). Pack a picnic and make the drive up Little Cottonwood Canyon to Alta, and enjoy the meadows full of mountain daisies, Indian paintbrush, and bluebells. Pretty much the greatest hits of alpine flowers are on display every year. Try to go on a weekday, however, to avoid the crowds.

Albion Basin, Alta
Broads Fork: Mill B South Trailhead, Big Cottonwood Canyon

TIP

If you're up for a strenuous hike and want to ditch the crowds altogether, the meadow at the top of Broads Fork is another of Utah's best wildflower areas. The hike, which starts in Big Cottonwood Canyon, is a four-plus mile beast, but you'll likely have the meadow up top all to yourself.

EXPLORE
A NATIONAL MONUMENT
IN DANGER

In Utah's southeasternmost reaches lies a land of secrets thinly veiled—vast wilderness where an ancient people once lived and thrived. Beyond every corner of every canyon lingers the anticipation of discovery, and the air hangs heavy with ghosts.

But this place, one of the most beautiful on earth, has been caught in a political struggle. Among his last acts in office, President Barack Obama declared this place—and all the ancient sites it holds—Bears Ears National Monument. Among his first acts in office, President Donald Trump undeclared it.

Bears Ears—named for two large, topographical landmarks that resemble, yes, a bear's ears—is on Cedar Mesa. Its appeal, however, isn't just scenic. Seven hundred to twenty-five hundred years ago, Cedar Mesa was home to a thriving civilization of cliff-dwelling people known as the Ancestral Puebloans and contemporaneously as Anasazi Indians. The latter name, which means "ancient ones" in Navajo, still is commonly used although it's not culturally accurate because the Navajo aren't related to these folks and the Pueblo are.

These people thrived between 800 and 1200 AD in a relatively peaceful and organized society, influenced by the same group that lived in Mesa Verde over in Colorado under the influence of a theorized HQ based in Chaco Canyon.

Most of this area is on public lands, lightly administered by the Bureau of Land Management (BLM), which is frantically trying to protect and preserve the ancient sites. But while the lawsuits mount and the battle rages on, there's no reason not to explore it on your own.

HOW TO GO

San Juan County is a five- to six-hour drive from Salt Lake City. Both Monticello and Bluff, Utah, make good bases of operation, and the surrounding area is mostly public lands with ample opportunities for camping. Be aware, however, that camping conditions are primitive, offering very few amenities.

The BLM has a field office in Monticello on Utah Highway 191, and the Kane Gulch Ranger Station—open from 8 a.m. to noon daily from March 1 through June 15 and September 1 through October 3— is located in the heart of the Mesa. Both are excellent resources for information and backcountry permits.

CHANT ALONG
AT A REAL SALT LAKE GAME

Major League Soccer is officially a thing, and Real Salt Lake (pronounced ree-Al) is one of the best teams in the US. Watching a match (not a game, silly) at Rio Tinto Stadium is an intense experience; the twenty-thousand-seat arena throbs with the exuberance of rabid Real supporters. Adopting the traditions of the European leagues, RSL fans employ a complicated system of chants and songs to cheer on the boys in claret and cobalt. Do your homework at realsaltlake.com before you head out to a match, and you'll fit right in.

Rio Tinto Stadium, 9256 S State St., Sandy, 801-727-2700
realsaltlake.com

ESCAPE
TO CITY CREEK CANYON

A true gem of escape, City Creek Canyon is mere minutes away from downtown Salt Lake City, where you can leave it all behind on a stroll up the canyon's paved road. The road goes six miles back into the foothills of Salt Lake and, apart from some water-treatment facilities, is entirely undeveloped. At the top, the Salt Lake Rotary Club has built some supercool picnic areas, including one called the Grotto on the shores of the babbling City Creek. Bikes are welcome on odd days in the summer and every day in the winter as well as leashed dogs. You'll find runners and bikers and walkers all taking a moment to step out of the city and find a little peace.

City Creek Canyon, City Creek Canyon Rd., Salt Lake City

"SPELUNK"
TIMPANOGOS CAVE

A national monument, Timpanogos Cave is just an hour from Salt Lake City. The ranger-led cave tours take place after a steep, 1.5-mile hike and often sell out, so book early. The climb is worth it; the wondrous Timpanogos Cave, an ancient cavern with stunning crystals called "frostwork," and the requisite stalactites and stalagmites live up to its monument status.

2038 Alpine Loop Rd., American Fork, 801-756-5239
nps.gov/tica/

TIP
Explore the Alpine Loop—a scenic byway near Mount Timpanogos and one of the best places to enjoy the fall colors in Utah.

TAKE A DOG
TO DOG LAKE

Having a dog (yours or a friend's) as a hiking buddy is pretty much the rule around here, and although some of our canyons (Big and Little Cottonwood) are off limits to canines (we get our drinking water from the snow up there), Millcreek Canyon is agnostic species-wise. You can find many great hikes in Millcreek, but perhaps none is more popular on an off-leash day (odd calendar days) than the trek back to Dog Lake. The moderately strenuous six-mile hike leads dogs and their owners to a good-sized muddy lake, where the pups can frolic while owners take their ease on the shore. Please, please, please pick up after your mutt.

Millcreek Canyon, Big Water Trailhead, Salt Lake City

DRIVE
THE MIRROR LAKE HIGHWAY

Pointing east from Kamas through the Uinta-Wasatch-Cache National Forest, the Mirror Lake Highway is a gorgeous high-mountain drive through some of the most stunning scenery in Utah. The road begins in the farm and ranch lands outside Kamas and rises into heavily forested, mountain terrain, accented by meadows and the rugged peaks of the Uinta range. The road is access to the camping and recreation areas dotting the mountains. Take a drive or go camping.

Heber-Kamas Ranger District, 50 E Center St., Kamas, 435-783-4338
435-783-4338

TIP
A campground bedazzled with dozens of "fairy homes" is located at mile marker 17 on the Mirror Lake Highway. It's the perfect place to stop with the little ones and watch them discover treasures left by mysterious fairies.

SPEND A SUNDAY AFTERNOON
AT THE BALLPARK

A lazy Sunday afternoon, the crack of the bat, the quiet murmur of the crowd, a cold beer, and a dog. Salt Lake has one of the best minor league ballparks in America, and here's a secret: the Sunday day games are pretty well empty. Baseball is a pastime after all, America's pastime. The local AAA farm club of the Los Angeles Angels, the Salt Lake Bees, have good years and bad, but who cares? The ballpark looks right up at the gorgeous mountains above the city, and you won't pay much for a ticket. Sit in the sun and while away the day while the boys of summer chase their major league dreams.

Smith's Ballpark, 77 W 1300 S, Salt Lake City, 801-350-6900
saltlake.bees.milb.com

TIP
Throughout the summer, night games are often punctuated by fireworks displays in the skies above the ballpark.

SCALE THE HEIGHTS
OF MOUNT OLYMPUS

Call it an initiation or even self-imposed hazing, but the slog to the summit of Mount Olympus (9,026 feet) is a necessary ritual on the path of calling yourself a hiker in Salt Lake. In our fair city, hiking, biking, and climbing are as endemic to life as navigating the subway is for a New Yorker. The grueling seven-mile-round-trip hike gains 4,196 feet in elevation, all on the exposed face of mighty Mount Olympus. It's a daunting task, and the giant rock stairs and scramble at the tippy top are a final twist of the dagger into your burning legs for sure. The reward, though, is the top-of-the-world panorama of the Central Wasatch Range and the Salt Lake Valley far, far below.

Mount Olympus Trailhead, 5800 S and Wasatch Blvd., Holladay

RIDE UP
EMIGRATION CANYON

Emigration Canyon is named for the Mormon pioneers who used the canyon to descend into the Salt Lake Valley. To mark the moment when the weary pioneers emerged from the canyon to observe their new home, LDS leader Brigham Young, famously declared, "This is the place." Nowadays, the canyon is prime real estate and lousy with road cyclists, who make the ascent to Little Mountain, at the top, in droves. It's a perfect road ride, with a wide shoulder, cyclist-conscious drivers, and a steady climb. The tamest of Salt Lake's canyon routes, it's an excellent introduction to the sport. The very top of the ride features a steep set of switchbacks that reward riders with a view of the valley below and a not-too-steep descent back down.

Emigration Canyon, Salt Lake City

FLOAT
THE WEBER RIVER

About an hour's drive north of Salt Lake City proper, you access the Weber River from the top of Ogden Canyon. Several guide companies offer shuttle services and tube and raft rentals, but you can really do this one on your own; plan for a shuttle car and some burly tubes that can withstand the rocks and tree branches. The two-hour float is a rowdy affair—most people bring an extra tube to float a cooler full of beer alongside—but the water itself is pretty mellow and shallow, with only a few tricky areas to navigate. You can get out and jump off rocks into deep pools in several spots, and a local landowner annually installs a giant rope swing for the truly brave souls in your flotilla.

TIP
As an alternative option, the Provo River is also a great river float. Several guide companies provide shuttle services and tubes. There is, however, one gnarly bridge you have to go under; heed your guide's warning and get out and walk around. High Country Adventure offers guide, shuttle, and rental services on both the Provo and Weber Rivers.

High Country Adventure, 3702 E Provo Canyon Rd., Provo, 801-224-2500
highcountryadventure.com

TAKE THE TRAM
TO HIDDEN PEAK

It's a quintessential Utah thing to do, especially for nonhikers in your world. The iconic red-and-blue trams will whisk you from the tram deck up to Hidden Peak, where you'll find spectacular views of the rugged Alpine peaks of the Wasatch Range and can peer down upon Salt Lake City. The newly constructed Summit Lodge offers shelter and lunch, and the second floor's height kicks the already jaw-dropping view up another notch. In the summer, you can hike down to the base or hike into (and out of, be warned) Mineral Basin. In late June and July, the wildflowers are a riot of color and beauty.

Snowbird Tram, 9385 S Snowbird Center Dr., Snowbird, 801-933-2222
snowbird.com

TIP
The hike up under the tram by the Snowbird trail system is a bugaboo, but the steep climb from eighty-one hundred feet to eleven thousand feet above sea level is a rewarding journey. Snowbird doesn't like to advertise this, but with a friendly wink for the tram operators, you can ride down for free as a reward for making the climb.

SEE A BISON,
EAT A BISON AT ANTELOPE ISLAND

The largest island in Great Salt Lake, Antelope Island is another world. The arid island, accessed by a causeway from I-15, is a lovely place to roam and disappear from the city. The views from the west side of the island out across the lake are a glimpse back in time before the works of man cluttered up the scenery.

What to do? Well, there's a herd of bison roaming around out there (and a restaurant that serves bison burgers sans irony), an excellent trail system, and several muddy beach areas to access the salty water. And the roads are heaven for cyclists.

Antelope Island State Park is located approximately forty-one miles north of Salt Lake City. Take Exit 332 off Interstate 15, and then drive west on Antelope Drive to the park entrance gate.

801-725-9263
stateparks.utah.gov/parks/antelope-island

TIP

Early spring, fall, and winter are the best times to visit. Summertime is hot, and what the island offers in stark beauty is offset by a noticeable lack of shade, and then you have bugs. Brine flies are prevalent in the warmer weather and pretty awful. They bite and leave painful, itchy welts. Call the park to ask if the flies have hatched. An excellent way to see the island is the annual Antelope by Moonlight Ride in July, a twenty-mile organized bike ride beneath the full moon.

antelopebymoonlight.com

LEARN TO SKI
(OR SNOWBOARD)

Salt Lake City is the base of six (six!) world-famous ski resorts: Alta, Snowbird, Brighton, Solitude, Park City, and Deer Valley. All are less than forty-five minutes from your door, and living in (or visiting) Utah and not skiing or snowboarding is like living in California and never going to the beach. We've got a skier on our license plates, for heck's sake.

So take a lesson. Even if you're a great skier or boarder, a lesson is a great way to tune up your technique. Do not let your boyfriend or girlfriend try to teach you. This situation is a relationship killer (believe me, I know). All six of the Salt Lake–area resorts have excellent ski-school programs and affordable lessons.

1-800-SKI-UTAH
skiutah.com

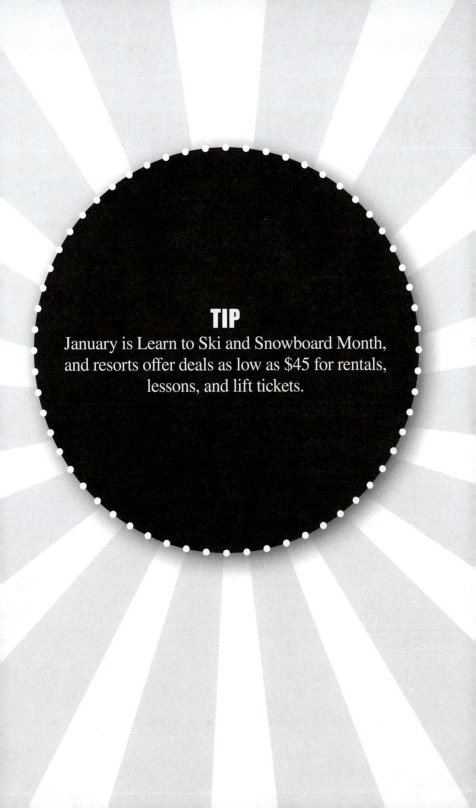

TIP

January is Learn to Ski and Snowboard Month, and resorts offer deals as low as $45 for rentals, lessons, and lift tickets.

HOW 'BOUT THAT JAZZ?

The Utah Jazz have been slugging it out in a rebuilding phase for a while. But new talent, coaching, and a facelift for their home arena complete with gargantuan jumbo screens make things seem like they're looking up. And we'll always have our memories of the glory days when John Stockton and Karl Malone were going toe-to-toe with Michael Jordan's Bulls. That's why long-suffering Jazz fans are among the most supportive and vociferous in the NBA, which makes every game a raucous, exciting event.

A word about the team's name: the Jazz used to be the NBA club in New Orleans. The team moved to Utah, complete with its Mardi Gras–laced name.

Vivint Smart Home Arena, 301 South Temple, Salt Lake City, 801-325-2000
nba.com/jazz

TIP

Stop into Tin Angel for a pregame dinner. Former SLC punkers Jerry Liedtke (Chef), Kestrel Liedtke (Heart& Soul) throw down a locally sourced menu of tasty food in a singularly cool atmosphere located near the arena.

Tin Angel, 365 W 400 S, Salt Lake City, 801-328-4155
thetinangel.com

THAT'LL DO, PIG,
ERR, DOG

Remember Babe, the pig who thought he was a dog? (Don't lie. You've seen *Babe*, like, a million times.) The Soldier Hollow Classic Sheepdog Trial Championship in Heber Valley is basically *Babe* without the pig. Contestants come from around the globe to show off their dogs' herding skills, which are impressive even if you're not a shepherd (or a talking pig).

The four-day event, one of the biggest of its kind in the world, is held over Labor Day weekend. It also features a vast array of dog-centric activities, such as the popular Splash Dogs competition, where water dogs go for distance, leaping into a pool chasing (what else?) a tennis ball. Note: Unless your four-legged friends are competing, you're asked to leave the pooches at home to avoid distracting the professionals.

2002 Soldier Hollow Ln., Midway, 435-654-2002
soldierhollowclassic.com

TIP

Make a getaway weekend out of the sheepdog trials, and book a room early at the nearby Zermatt Resort and Spa or Homestead Resort. Spend the last weekend of summer in the beautiful Heber Valley, enjoying the pampering *and* pooches.

WALK
AMONG THE ICE CASTLES

The Midway Ice Castles are constructed each year out of soaring walls of frozen water to the delight of bundled-up adults and children, who walk through the maze-like structure in droves every winter. The wondrous playground is built when the cold really sets in and is naturally weather dependent. Buy tickets in advance, get a thermos of hot cocoa, and take the kids for a cold-weather adventure.

Midway Ice Castles, 2002 Soldier Hollow Rd., Midway, 866-435-2850
icecastles.com/midway

SKATE
ON THE FASTEST ICE ON EARTH

Many of the records set in speed skating during the 2002 Winter Games in Salt Lake City still stand today. The Utah Olympic Oval is a training center for future Olympians, but you need not be one of those to enjoy the beautiful rink. It offers public skating as well as a great place to watch athletes in training, international speed skating events, and more. Come winter, the indoor running track attracts runners who want to avoid the cold.

Utah Olympic Oval, 5662 Cougar Ln., Kearns, 801-968-6825
utaholympiclegacy.org/oval/

CELEBRATE THE SOLSTICE
AT THE SUN TUNNELS

Land artist Nancy Holt installed the sun tunnels in 1978 in the western desert near Lucin, Utah. The four massive concrete tubes aren't much to look at in the light of day, but during the summer and winter solstice, the tunnels frame the sun at sunrise and sunset. For each astrophysical event, a motley assemblage of nature lovers, art lovers, weirdos, and wanderers camp out around the tunnels for an all-night party to witness the events.

Sun Tunnels, Lucin

SOAK YOUR BONES
AT FIFTH WATER HOT SPRINGS

Enough of a hike to keep out the casual but not enough of a trek to deter interesting folks, Fifth Water Hot Springs is located in Diamond Fork Canyon. You'll hike five miles out and back to the springs, which pour into a series of pools that are hottest near the source. It's an excellent excursion in either winter or summer. But be prepared that hot springs in the West are often clothing optional, so you may encounter a bare behind or two. Feel free to bare your own.

Fifth Water Hot Springs, Diamond Fork Canyon, 801-798-3571

TAKE A ROAD TRIP
TO RED ROCK COUNTRY

Southern Utah's stunning red-rock deserts are the exact opposite of the north's mountainous landscape. Salt Lake City is within five hours' drive of some of the world's most amazing places of solitude and splendor. You're not a real Salt Laker until you've ducked out of work early on a Friday (don't let them hear your keys jingling), loaded up the car, and made the trek down south for the weekend. In addition to the five national parks within Utah's borders, there are numerous state parks and national monuments, lovely little towns, and miles of wide open spaces. Here are some highlights:

MOAB
Distance from SLC: 234 miles

A base of operations for exploring nearby Arches and Canyonlands National Parks as well as Dead Horse Point State Park. Moab is also close to the famous (and dangerous) Slickrock Trail mountain biking area.

GOBLIN VALLEY STATE PARK
Distance from SLC: 223 miles

This state park is home to a preponderance of red-rock "goblins." The mushroom-like products of incomplete erosion create a wondrous maze of weirdness to wander through.

SPRINGDALE

Distance from SLC: 307 miles

This cute little town is the entrance to Zion National Park and a great base for exploring the region. Nearby St. George and Cedar City offer year-round golfing (St. George) and the Tony Award–winning Utah Shakespeare Festival (Cedar City).

BOULDER, ESCALANTE, AND SCENIC HIGHWAY 12

Distance from SLC: 306 miles

Bryce Canyon and Capitol Reef National Parks as well as the Grand Staircase–Escalante National Monument are all along this off-the-beaten-path roadway. Don't miss a reservations-required dinner at the famous Hell's Backbone Grill in Boulder.

LAKE POWELL

Distance from SLC: 383 miles

Formed by Glen Canyon Dam, this reservoir has more miles of knotted-up coastline than the western edge of the United States and is a strange watery oasis in the middle of the harsh desert.

CULTURE AND HISTORY

CAMP OUT
FOR THE PARADE

The Days of '47 is the annual celebration of Pioneer Day (July 24), the day the LDS settlers entered the valley. The annual parade on or around that date, depending on when the weekend falls, is a Utah tradition. Families camp out on the parade route to ensure a prime spot. The parade is, well, a parade, but the camping is a wholesome all-nighter on the city streets. And this isn't just chairs and blankets; people go big, with generators, blow-up mattresses, and much more.

801-257-7959
daysof47.com

GET A DOSE
OF "UTAH WEIRD" AT
GILGAL SCULPTURE GARDEN

Gilgal Sculpture Garden was the backyard of Thomas Battersby Child Jr., a businessman and mason who died in 1963. The bizarre folk art sculptures dot a quiet little park nestled in a Salt Lake neighborhood. The themes are often LDS-centric, notably the giant sphinx bearing the likeness of LDS Church founder Joseph Smith. The park is open to the public daily.

Gilgal Sculpture Garden, 749 E 500 S, Salt Lake City, 801-972-7860
gilgalgarden.org

SEE
HISTORIC TEMPLE SQUARE

On July 24, 1847, the weary Mormon pioneers arrived in the Salt Lake Valley, but their leader, Brigham Young, didn't let them rest long. They got busy, real busy. Just four days after they arrived, they marked the spot to build the Salt Lake Temple. Construction took forty-six years, and early Salt Lake City grew up around it. Now you can say, literally, that all roads lead to Temple Square (the city's grid system counts out on the compass points from here). The iconic, granite-spired structure is the centerpiece of the grounds that pack in some of Utah's densest history lessons. There's a lot to do at Temple Square, as well as the adjacent LDS Church Headquarters Plaza and Conference Center. At a minimum, take an hour and stroll through the beautiful, intensely manicured grounds. It is—whatever your faith, creed, or culture— a place of peace in the heart of the city.

Temple Square, 50 N Temple, Salt Lake City, 801-531-1000
lds.org/locations/salt-lake-city-temple-square

TEMPLE SQUARE MUST-DOS

Hear the Pin Drop

The historic Mormon Tabernacle, in use since 1898 and home to the Mormon Tabernacle Choir, is an acoustic marvel. Tours include the famous pin drop, in which your group can clearly hear a pin being dropped up front while standing in back.

Tour the Beehive House

One of Brigham Young's stately homes is open for tours. Yes, Brigham was a polygamist, and his homes had many, many rooms for his many, many wives. Take the tour and be rewarded with a glimpse into Utah's peculiar past and a taste of what pioneer candy tasted like (not good).

Go to the 26th Floor

Once the tallest building in Salt Lake, the LDS Church office building is the worldwide administrative headquarters of the church. An observation deck on the 26th floor offers a commanding view of the city and a unique view of the top of the Salt Lake Temple.

Hear the Mormon Tabernacle Choir for Free

Every Sunday morning, the Mormon Tabernacle Choir is featured in a live devotional broadcast called *Music and the Spoken Word*. Tickets to the weekly broadcast are free. The broadcast location switches between the original historic tabernacle in the winter and the larger LDS Conference Center (we call it the "Supernacle") during summer to accommodate larger crowds.

Here Comes the Bride(s)

Young LDS Church members are directed to marry as a matter of doctrine, and the ceremony is held within the temple. Sit in the Main Street Plaza and watch the parade of modest young couples posing for postnuptial pictures on the temple's steps.

See the Christmas Lights

On the day after Thanksgiving, the Christmas lights come on at Temple Square, and it just wouldn't be the holidays without a stroll through the lights. Millions of lights are strung beginning in August, and the display is a sparkly celebration of the season.

SEE THE STARS
AND MAYBE A GREAT FILM AT
THE SUNDANCE FILM FESTIVAL

The big show happens in Park City, where celebrities promoting their films are often sighted clomping around historic Main Street in hastily purchased boots and winter clothes. Although the star-stalking thing is a thing, let's remember that Sundance is one of the world's most important independent film festivals. A cinephile's dream, the two-week festival is a buffet of films both little and big and always interesting. Although the crowds flock to Park City, film lovers know to stay down in Salt Lake, where the wait is tolerable and the celebrity circus less prominent.

310-360-1981
sundance.org/festivals/sundance-film-festival

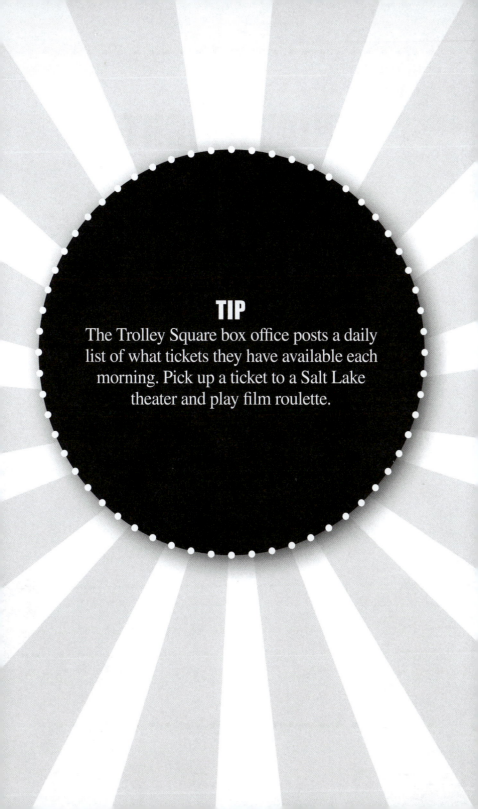

TIP

The Trolley Square box office posts a daily list of what tickets they have available each morning. Pick up a ticket to a Salt Lake theater and play film roulette.

ENJOY A NIGHT
AT THE THEATER

Salt Lake City has long been a culturally rich town boasting its resident Utah Symphony and Opera Company, and Ballet West, its world-renowned ballet troupe, and its residents rejoice in a celebration of theater. The Pioneer Theatre Company's proscenium is the grande dame of the stages here in Utah. Presenting an annual season that ranges across Shakespeare, musicals, and challenging works by Chekov, PMT is the top professional stage in Utah.

The newly minted George S. and Dolores Doré Eccles Theater is a state-of-the-art hall that attracts a wide variety of touring performances, including the latest and greatest from the Great White Way.

Pioneer Theatre Company, 300 S 1400 E, Salt Lake City, 801-581-6961
pioneertheatre.org

Eccles Theater, 131 S Main St., Salt Lake City, 385-468-1010
artsaltlake.org

STROLL PAST THE MANSIONS
ON SOUTH TEMPLE

One of Brigham Young's prescriptions for a healthy economy was forbidding his followers to seek out gold and other minerals in them thar hills. Remember, the LDS pioneers came here in 1847, and the California gold rush was in 1849. Brigham's logic was based on what he believed was the boom-bust nature of mining-based economies. Thus, it was left to outsiders to discover the wealth under the soil, and they did. In the late 1800s, a group of capitalists tapped into a rich vein of silver in the area that is now Park City, and they became very, very rich. The "silver barons," as they were called, built massive mansions on South Temple Street, one of which now serves as the Utah governor's home. Take a walk down the long tree-lined avenue.

South Temple between State Street and Virginia Avenue

TIP
The Utah Heritage Foundation offers guided tours of many of the historical homes on South Temple, tours of other historically and architecturally significant areas of SLC, and downloadable self-guided tours.

utahheritagefoundation.org

WAVE A RAINBOW FLAG
IN THE UTAH PRIDE PARADE

Being the home to the world headquarters of a conservative church brings out the oppositional defiance of nonbelievers. That tension, at times acrimonious, makes Salt Lake City a surprisingly liberal place despite its location in the heart of one of the reddest states in the Union. In 2015, Salt Lake voters elected Jackie Biskupski, the city's first openly gay mayor. The Salt Lake Pride Festival is perhaps the best example of this jubilant opposition, and the four-day festival is one of the largest of its kind in the nation (seriously). The celebration brings LGBT folks and their loving supporters out into the streets and culminates in a joyous parade through the heart of the city that rivals the annual Pioneer Day parade in participation and attendance.

Salt Lake Pride Festival, utahpridefestival.org

FLY THE HELICOPTER
AT DISCOVERY GATEWAY

Discovery Gateway is a children's museum, but *museum* is too boring a word. Think interactive exhibits and hands-on play areas that cater to kids and the kid inside all of us. The sixty-thousand-square-foot, multifloor play space features engaging workshops and programs, all centered around kid-powered fun. They also have this supercool helicopter on the roof, where you can pretend to rescue people, as well as a place where you can pretend to be on the news. And then you can pretend to go to the store and buy all the groceries. It's way awesome. Can we go? Can we go? Pleeease?

Discovery Gateway, 444 W 100 S, Salt Lake City, 801-456-5437
discoverygateway.org

MARVEL
AT *SPIRAL JETTY*

American sculptor Robert Smithson built *Spiral Jetty* in 1970. The giant sculpture on the northern tip of Great Salt Lake is what it says it is—a curly rock jetty that goes out into the lake. During wet years, the jetty is covered with water, but of late the beautiful rock sculpture is bone dry with a salty patina.

Spiral Jetty, Corinne

TIP

A trip out to Spiral Jetty is paired well with a visit to the Golden Spike National Historic Site, which commemorates the coming together of the eastern and western lines of the transcontinental railroad at Promontory Summit in 1869.

Golden Spike National Historic Site, 6200 N 22300 W, Brigham City
435-471-2209
nps.gov/gosp

TIME TRAVEL
AT THE NATURAL HISTORY MUSEUM OF UTAH

The interactive exhibits at the NHMU walk you through life in Utah—from rocks on up to the flora and fauna—and make it a standard educational field trip. The building itself is also reason enough for a visit. Its architecture recalls the slot canyons and rocks of southern Utah, and following the winding path through the museum takes you on a journey through the natural history of our state. But, yay! Dinosaurs! Lots of dinosaurs. Utah is one of the world's richest areas of dinosaur-fossil discovery, and the museum is home to impressive exhibits of skeletal giant reptiles from way, way back.

Natural History Museum of Utah, 301 Wakara Way, Salt Lake City
801-581-6927
nhmu.utah.edu

TELL YOUR STORY
AT THE BEE

In 2014, Salt Laker Giuliana Serena founded The Bee, monthly storytelling competitions inspired by The Moth in New York City. The Bee—which is a nod to Utah's nickname, The Beehive State—has been going strong ever since. Serena has dubbed the events "evenings of lovingly competitive storytelling," and each night features ten local storytellers whose names have been drawn at random from a hat.

There's always a clever topic—"Grit: Stories of courage, resolve, and strength of character," for example. The stories must be true; ideally, have a beginning, a middle, and an end (no post-structuralism here, please); and be told without notes in under five minutes. Guest judges in the audience score the stories, but the competition is really just a side note to the wonderful tales from amateurs with something to share.

Tickets to the monthly events go fast; so be sure to sign up for the email list so you get alerts when they go on sale and details on the changing locations. Themes are announced in advance of each show, along with a call for stories from willing volunteers. But you can also sign up the night-of. Be brave and tell your tale. And before you go, take a dive into the archives on their website, where you'll even find a story by this brave author.

The Bee, Salt Lake City
thebeeslc.org

BONUS

The Bee also offers workshops for anyone looking to work on their storytelling skills, even those who never want to get on stage. Sessions of *Storytelling for Grown-Ups* happen throughout the year. Check The Bee's website for the next one.

CHECK THE SKYLINE
WEATHER REPORT

Walker Center, built in 1912, is one of Salt Lake's grand old edifices. Its distinctive lighted top broadcasts a weather report every evening. Put down your phone, look up, and use this key to the code: blue = clear skies, flashing blue = cloudy skies, red = rain, flashing red = snow.

Walker Center, 175 South Main St., Salt Lake City, 801-521-0415

GO UP (DOWN?)
GRAVITY HILL

The one-way road that runs around the edge of the mouth of City Creek Canyon is a strange optical illusion that is a source of whimsy, especially for bike riders who use the road's large bike lane. The road seems to be going downhill, but you'll be pedaling hard because you're actually going uphill. The opposite effect occurs on the west side of the road.

Gravity Hill, City Creek Canyon Rd., Salt Lake City

ORDER A DRINK
AT BUTCH AND SUNDANCE'S BAR

The Sundance Kid is perhaps Robert Redford's most iconic role. The famous actor is certainly fond of his turn alongside Paul Newman in the 1969 film *Butch Cassidy and the Sundance Kid*, so much so that he named his ski resort and the world-renowned independent film festival after the character.

The character Sundance, in turn, was based on the real-life exploits of Harry Longabaugh, who along with Robert LeRoy Parker, AKA Butch Cassidy, were part of the Hole in the Wall Gang, a loose consortium of outlaws who operated out of hideout in Johnson County, Wyoming. The various gang members rustled cattle and horses, robbed banks, stagecoaches, and, as depicted in the film, trains. The train heists brought down the wrath of the Union Pacific Railroad bosses who dispatched the infamous Pinkertons to dispatch the outlaws. The Pinkertons chased Butch and Sundance into South America where the duo is thought to have died in 1908 in Bolivia in a shootout with soldiers.

The Hole in the Wall hideout was near Thermopolis, Wyoming, where the Rosewood Bar was frequented by Butch Cassidy the Sundance Kid. Redford started building Sundance in 1968 and has worked to maintain a certain refined rusticity at the ski and snowboarding area. When building the central lodge area, his designers purchased the Rosewood's wooden bar and backing and had it shipped to Utah. It was carefully reassembled and is now the centerpiece of the ski village's main watering hole, the Owl Bar. So be sure to belly up and order a glass of whiskey to toast Butch and the Sundance Kid.

Memory Grove, 75 N 120 E, Salt Lake City
slcparks.com

TIP

After you've enjoyed a glass or two at the Owl Bar, try out Sundance's Zip Tour, a year-round thrill ride that features a 2,100-foot vertical drop, which makes it 100 percent scarier than any other zip line tour in the United States, in my opinion.

HYDRATE
WITH HISTORY

When the Mormon pioneers arrived in the Salt Lake Valley, finding water was top of mind. Early on, a natural spring was discovered at what is now the corner of Salt Lake's best urban green space, Liberty Park. The spring was corralled into a drinking fountain that runs year-round and is a refreshing treat after a run in the park or a game of tag on the grassy knoll. Explore the rest of the park, and be sure to notice Seven Canyons Fountain, which will give you an excellent sense of the valley's topography. Also check out the Live Action Role Players (LARPers), who practice their broadsword skills on the grass.

Liberty Park, 600 E 900 S, Salt Lake City
https://www.slc.gov/parks/parks-division/liberty-park

FIND THE
TWO-HEADED LAMB
AT THE DUP MUSEUM

The Daughters of Utah Pioneers Museum on Capitol Hill is a great place to learn the history of the women and families who, in many cases, literally walked across the Great Plains to settle Utah in 1847. The museum tells a gentler side of that history and gives a glimpse into what family life was like on the trek. It's also (whaaa?) the home of a strange taxidermied two-headed lamb. Happy hunting!

Daughters of Utah Pioneers Museum, 300 Main St., Salt Lake City
801-532-6479
dupinternational.org

DISCOVER "THE PLACE"
AT THIS IS THE PLACE STATE PARK

You may have guessed that the Mormon settlement of Salt Lake City is a very big deal around here. Apart from Temple Square, perhaps the most important LDS history site is This Is the Place State Park. A monument marks the spot where Brigham Young intoned the famous words and allowed his followers to finally park their wagons and handcarts. You can just imagine the collective sigh of relief.

The park has historical buildings, a trove of history, and docents who practice lost arts such as blacksmithing and woodworking. Kids can play pioneer games (that are pretty fun, actually).

This Is the Place State Park, 2601 E Sunnyside Ave., Salt Lake City
801-582-1847
thisistheplace.org

CLIMB THE STAIRS
AT THE SALT LAKE CITY PUBLIC LIBRARY

Oh, man, our library. Designed by internationally acclaimed architect Moshe Safdie, the city library is a beautiful public space: the soaring main hall, the beautiful plaza with fountains, the light streaming in the plentiful windows. The grand steps encircle the eastern flank of the building, and a walk up the stairs offers a lovely view of the city as well as access to the library's rooftop gardens (with a resident beehive). Take the glass elevator back down and look at books, read a magazine, plug in to the free Wi-Fi (I wrote much of this book on the library's third floor), browse the library shops, or just slow down and enjoy this wonderful space.

Salt Lake City Public Library, 210 E 400 S, Salt Lake City, 801-524-8200
slcpl.org/branches/view/Main+Library

LOOK UP
FOR FLYING OBJECTS

Salt Lake's city center is dotted with an ongoing public art project called *Flying Objects*. The whimsical sculptures are installed on poles near Salt Lake's main cultural halls. A local favorite is Brook Robertson's *Zion/Alien Rocky Mountain Alliance 4.4* at the Rose Wagner Performing Arts Center, which features a pair of LDS missionaries behind the wheel of a Jetsons-style flying saucer.

Abravanel Hall: 10 S West Temple, Salt Lake City
Rose Wagner Performing Arts Center: 125 W 300 S, Salt Lake City
Capitol Theatre: 15 W 200 S, Salt Lake City

SEE A SILENT FILM
WITH FULL ORGAN ACCOMPANIMENT

The Edison Street Events Center, historically known as the Organ Loft, is home to a full-on Wurlitzer theatre pipe organ that was once state of the art in movie soundtracks. The reception hall offers periodic showings of silent-film classics, accompanied by the magnificently maintained organ. The most popular of these is the annual October showing of *The Phantom of the Opera*.

Edison Street Events Center, 3331 S Edison St. (145 E), Salt Lake City
801-485-9265
edisonstreetevents.com

SHOPPING AND FASHION

DIG THROUGH THE DESIGNER SECTION
AT NPS

A through-the-looking-glass closeout, scratch and dent, ultimate end of the road for any item that was once sold for full price somewhere in the world, NPS (standing generically for National Product Sales) is a clearance sale, every day. But in the middle of this daily fire-sale chaos is a special designer section. These are real deals, not knockoffs—Coach bags, Jimmy Choo shoes, TAG Heuer watches. The selection changes constantly (except for some very odd decorating items that will be there forever). You pretty much have to pick through everything, but once in a while you'll pay an insanely low price for that perfect dress, watch, shoes, or umm, heirloom cuckoo clock.

NPS, 1600 Empire Rd., Salt Lake City, 801-972-4132
npsstore.com

FIND THAT
SOMETHING SPECIAL
AT TABULA RASA

When I was working up new entries for this second edition, I was kicking myself for not including Tabula Rasa, a Salt Lake Institution in the inaugural book. Every great city has a great stationers, and Tabula Rasa most certainly is the place to go to order special invitations, note cards, engravings, and all that society stuff.

To me, though, it's so much more. Owner Sean Bradley, a man of elegance and taste whose typical dress is an impeccable suit and tie, stocks his shop with curious and precious items from around the globe. His store is the place to go for that extra-special gift for that extra-special someone on those occasions when you just can't for the life of you think what your extra-special someone would love and you are extra-especially stumped.

Tabula Rasa, 330 Trolley Square, Salt Lake City, 801-575-5043
tabularasastationers.com

TIP
La Rasa, as we locals call it (jokingly butchering the Latin for *blank page*,) stocks beautiful calendars for the new year. Many of us locals wouldn't consider starting a new year without one of these calendars, so go in September or October for the pick of litter.

UPGRADE YOUR SPECS
AT THE SPECTACLE

For more than three decades, Salt Lakers who sport glasses have known to look here for that special pair of specs. Remember the signature glasses worn by Elvis that you probably just call "Elvis glasses"? Owner John Cottom designed those as well as the heart-shaped eyewear famously worn by actress Ann-Margret. His handiwork can also be seen in the sci-fi classic *Blade Runner*. The Spectacle also carries lots of cool vintage glasses and hard-to-find designer brands.

Spectacle, 330 Trolley Square, Salt Lake City, 801-359-2020
thespectacle.com

SHOP FOR THE KIDS (AND MOM)
AT THE CHILDREN'S HOUR

The name sounds like it's a toy store or a kids' bookshop, right? The Children's Hour, located in the hip 9th and 9th district of Salt Lake City, has an interesting and thoughtful selection of children's books, educational toys, and the oh-so-cutest clothing for the little ones. But it has hard-to-find brands of shoes, handbags, and clothing for mom, too. Also, there are cute cards and other gifts for everyone. And if you need something, say, a little on the naughty side, just walk across the street to Cahoots for a selection of adult-themed gifts.

The Children's Hour, 898 S 900 E, Salt Lake City, 801-359-4150
childrenshourbookstore.com

Cahoots, 878 S 900 S, Salt Lake City, 801-538-0606
cahootssaltlake.com

PERUSE KEN SANDERS
RARE BOOKS

Ken Sanders Rare Books is one of those special places that can exist only because of the personality of its owner. Ken Sanders is a counter-culture icon in Utah. His locally focused rare and used bookstore is a veritable museum of Utah history and a repository for the works of such great Utah writers as Wallace Stegner and Edward Abbey. But it's also so much more. His store holds a wonderful collection of old maps, rock 'n' roll concert posters, and postcards from fin de siècle Salt Lake City.

In addition to Sanders' store, Salt Lake is home to The King's English Bookshop, an institution run by matriarch (and author in her own right) Betsy Burton. The small store thinks big and regularly hosts big-name signings and author events (including for yours truly) in addition to being just the cutest little store in just the cutest little neighborhood. Check their calendar for upcoming events, and plan your evening around a book chat and dinner at one of four(!) neighboring local restaurants: Mazza (Middle Eastern), Paris Bistro (French), Caputo's (Italian deli), or Trestle Tavern (American bistro).

Ken Sanders Rare Books, 268 S 200 E, Salt Lake City, 801-521-3819
kensandersbooks.com

The King's English Bookshop, 1511 S 1500 E, Salt Lake City
801-484-9100
kingsenglish.com

GET LOST
IN DECADES

It's almost like the staff who stalk the floor at Decades Vintage Clothing love their beautifully curated collection of threads so much they'd rather you *not* buy it. But their brisk service is part of the charm of this sprawling store on State Street, where you'll find a treasure trove of midcentury gems, jewelry, hats, shoes, and much more. The staff's aloof attitude tells you that this place isn't about playing dress up; it's about fine goods and timeless fashion.

Decades, 627 S State St., Salt Lake City, 801-537-1357

ANARCHY
IN SLC

Salt Lake City, unexpectedly, was heavy into the punk thing during the Reagan era. While most of the country was rehabbing at Betty Ford and marching lockstep into the new "morning in America," the scruffy underground was busy saying "no" to saying "no," breaking things, and being generally mad and loud. Salt Lake City upped this anti-everything vibe with an extra sheen of squeaky-clean Mormon and bred an especially virulent antibody to the cultural vaccine, *SLC Punk!* Two vestiges of this period live on at Raunch Records and the Heavy Metal Shop (motto: "Peddling evil since 1987"), both of which sell vinyl and angry memorabilia from back in the days of anarchy in SLC.

Raunch Records, 1119 E 2100 S, Salt Lake City, 801-467-6077

Heavy Metal Shop, 63 S Exchange Pl., Salt Lake City, 801-467-7071
heavymetalshop.com

SHOP
AT NINTH AND NINTH

Ninth and Ninth is a cool neighborhood shopping and dining area anchored by Tower Theatre. You'll find hipster clothing shops; the town's highest-end bike shop, Contender; and The Children's Hour, the little gem that sells smart books and toys for the kids as well as hard-to-find designer clothing brands and gifts for mom. Stop in Zuriick for a pair of handmade shoes and a haircut, and head to Cahoots for whimsical gifts and adult toys. Take a lunch break at Mazza, serving Lebanese cuisine, or East Liberty Tap House, serving beer and a solid menu including one of the city's best burgers.

900 S 900 E, Salt Lake City, 385-209-0220
9thand9th.com

SCORE A DEAL
AT THE SUNDANCE CATALOG OUTLET STORE

C'mon. Your coffee table has an earmarked Sundance catalog on it, right? The catalog—featuring unique clothing, jewelry, and housewares inspired by Robert Redford's haute western aesthetic—has an outlet store here in Salt Lake. This is a true outlet; the markdowns are legit and often steep.

Sundance Catalog Outlet Store, 2201 S Highland Dr., Salt Lake City
1-800-422-2770
sundancecatalog.com

WINDOW SHOP
AT UTAH'S TIFFANY

Utah's original jeweler has been putting beautiful baubles on people for nearly a century. And even if you're not in the market for fine jewelry, stopping in its flagship store on State Street is worth the trip. The store is located in the former Salt Lake City Public Library Building, beautifully renovated into a gorgeous space filled with gorgeous jewelry.

O.C. Tanner Jewelers, 15 S State St., Salt Lake City, 801-532-3222
octannerjewelers.com

BE A KID AGAIN
IN JITTERBUG ANTIQUES & TOYS

Crowd into a delightfully curated consignment store of retro goods and an impressive menagerie of toys and games from days of yore. With its windup tin toys, Jitterbug Antiques is a chattering, whimsical wonderland and an excellent spot to find nostalgia-inspiring gifts.

Jitterbug Antiques & Toys, 243 E 300 S, Salt Lake City, 801-537-7038

DIVE FOR BARGAINS
AT DESERET INDUSTRIES

You probably think of Goodwill or the Salvation Army when you think thrift store, but we in Utah think Deseret Industries. Known as the D.I., this store has many locations around the valley, and diving through the stacks of clothes, books, housewares, and everything else is a rite of passage for college students furnishing their first apartments. Gems can sometimes be found amid the piles of polyester jumpsuits.

deseretindustries.org

GET YOUR MANE CUT
AT A BARBER SHOP

It all went to hell in the seventies. A generation's rejection of taciturn fathers, plastic-fantastic Madison Avenue, and the whole Military Industrial Complex was symbolized in long, untamed male hair. When that somehow became the system, barbers—sphinx-like keepers of masculine-follicle lore—were replaced by unisex salons and one-size-cut-all box shops. And a generation of American men was subjected to bad haircuts and a prickly, Matrix-like sensation that something was not right with their heads.

But the barbers hung on, like Knights Templar, hiding in plain sight, keeping the lore, training a clandestine army of young clippers to one day rise up and reclaim the hair of America's quietly desperate men. "Follow us," they cried, "and renounce frosted tips, waxed chests, cucumber water, and plinky flute music at the ladies' salon."

This renaissance is about beards, big beards. It's about perfect parts, tapered necklines, high-and-tight cuts that you can set your watch by. It's a long-overdue rejection of Joe Namath's feathered mane and a return to Johnny Unitas's bristles, close shaves, trimmed beards, and the haircuts of a generation tough enough to whip the Great Depression and global fascism with a Lucky Strike dangling from their lips.

Salt Lake City is part of this revival of barbering. On the next page are some of the best places to get that mane tamed.

The Barber School
In 2006, when Utah reinstated the barber license, The Barber School got off the ground in Midvale. Old-school barber Milt Larsen, who was asked to join the faculty, is proud to be passing on the tradition and training a new generation of barbers. A big plus: students give cuts for cheap.

16 W 7200 S, Midvale, 801-304-7000
thebarberschool.com

Cutthroat Barbershop
Located on Salt Lake's westside, Cutthroat has a very westside vibe, like a graffitied junkyard chop shop only for hair. Despite his gruff exterior, owner Mike Canales is a real sweetie.

2851 S Redwood Rd., West Valley City, 385-242-7523
cutthroatbarbershopslc.com

Garrett Micheal Barber Shop
Daniella Marquin came to Utah to be a barber. Her shop Garret Michael, named after her son, started small. Now Dani has a new, larger shop and a fiercely loyal clientele. Stop in for a killer cut and then drop into Dick 'n' Dixies, the neighborhood bar next door, for a pint.

435 E 300 S, Salt Lake City, 801-359-4580
gmbarbershop.com

Haircutter Too
At Haircutter Too, two generations man chairs and wield scissors and razors. Dad Al Fitzgerald resembles a refugee ski bum from the Jackson Brown-era seventies, still sporting the jeans and denim shirts harkening back to James Taylor on the cover of *Sweet Baby James*. Son Colby is basically the same make but the 2000s model, with ironic wrist-to-shoulder tattoos, a pierced nose, and hair whose color and length are ever-changing. The Eagles meets Kings of Leon.

10582 S 700 E, Sandy, 801-572-0562

The Razor and Dram
In Sugar House, around the back from a day care and down the stairs, is Josh Roh's Razor and Dram. Josh, who considers himself a "gentleman's gentleman," has created a den dedicated to manliness, complete with a rotating selection of old VHS horror and sci-fi movies on the tele in the corner.

1549 S 1100 E, Suite C, Salt Lake City, 801-867-6399
razoranddram.com

SUGGESTED
ITINERARIES

MORMON UTAH

Order up Some Lion House Rolls, 19

See a Concert in the "Supernacle," 57

Camp out for the Parade, 96

See Historic Temple Square, 98

Find the Two-Headed Lamb at the DUP Museum, 115

Discover "the Place" at This Is the Place State Park, 116

Deseret Industries, 133

WEIRD UTAH

Go to Theater That's Not *in* the Theater, 52

Rent *Rubin and Ed* at Tower Theatre, 54

Diving in the Desert? Scuba at Five Thousand Feet above
   Sea Level, 61

Choose Sides in the "Holy War," 64

Celebrate the Solstice at the Sun Tunnels, 90

Tell Your Story at The Bee, 108

Get a Dose of "Utah Weird" at Gilgal Sculpture Garden, 97

Wave a Rainbow Flag in the Utah Pride Parade, 104

Marvel at *Spiral Jetty*, 106

YES, YOU CAN GET A DRINK IN UTAH

LET THE MUSIC PLAY

OUTDOOR ADVENTURES

FAMILY FUN

ACTIVITIES
BY SEASON

Salt Lake City is a place with four clear seasons, some of the activities are season-specific or at their best during a particular time of year.

SPRING

Scale the Heights of Mount Olympus, 76

See a Bison, Eat a Bison at Antelope Island, 80

Go to Hell('s Backbone) in Boulder, 34

SUMMER

Take the Tram to Hidden Peak, 79

Tell Your Story at The Bee, 108

Get Dinner Fixings at the Downtown Farmers Market, 2

Eat a Brigham City Peach on Fruit Way, 22

Float the Weber River, 78

Camp out for the Parade, 96

Take the Train for Ogden Twilight, 40

Go to Theater That's Not *in* the Theater, 52

Spend the Day at Lagoon, 49

Paddle Outrigger Canoes on Great Salt Lake, 60

Go to Hell('s Backbone) in Boulder, 34

Picnic It Up at a Red Butte Show, 44

FALL

INDEX